The *ultimate* POTATO COOKBOOK

bay books

Duchess potatoes (top) and Hasselback potatoes, page 20

CONTENTS

The test kitchen is where our recipes are double-tested by our team of home economists to ensure a high standard of success and delicious results every time.

After testing, recipes are rated for ease of preparation and given one of the following cookery ratings in this book.

A single Cooking with Confidence symbol indicates that this recipe is simple and fairly quick to make, perfect for beginners.

Two symbols indicate the need for a little more care and time.

Three symbols indicate special dishes that require more time, care and patience, but the results are worth it.

Potatoes with Garlic Mayonnaise, page 25

Potatoes Anna, page 19

Clockwise, from left: Russet (Idaho), Purple Congo, King Edward, Desiree, Bintje, Nicola, Pink Eye, Pontiac

Potato varieties

The humble potato, now a staple part of the diet throughout much of the world, originated in South America where it has been cultivated for centuries. The Portuguese and Spanish transported potatoes to Europe in the 16th Century and probably introduced them to India as well. As a food crop, potatoes are cheap, hardy and easy to grow. They contain starch, protein and vitamins and therefore served as an excellent staple for the poor. The Irish came to rely on them so heavily that the potato blight of 1845–6 caused widespread famine and death. By the 18th Century, the potato was an important vegetable in Europe and has become the fourth most important food crop in the world after wheat, maize and rice.

Potatoes are remarkably versatile as they can be boiled, mashed, baked, fried, roasted or barbecued and can be made into bread, pancakes, soups, gratins, tarts and pies. There are more than 1000 different types of potato but only about 100 varieties are grown commercially. This is gradually changing with an increasing number of varieties being grown and becoming available. Correct labelling of each type is improving in the shops, making it easier for the consumer to choose appropriate ones for particular dishes. Some potatoes are good all-round types, others are more suitable for specific ways of cooking. In our recipes we refer to floury, waxy, new or salad potatoes. A recipe which simply asks for potatoes requires an all-purpose variety.

RUSSET (Idaho)
Long in shape, these floury potatoes are known as baking potatoes because that is how they are best prepared. Their high starch content also makes them good for French fries.

PURPLE CONGO
A purple, long oval potato which retains its colour when cooked. It is excellent for preparing gnocchi and mashing as the flesh is dry when cooked. Also good for making crisps and chips.

KING EDWARD
An English variety of floury potato with a creamy white flesh and a red blush on the end. Suitable for mashing, baking and chips, but not for boiling.

DESIREE
Waxy, long, oval, pink-skinned with creamy yellow flesh. Great for boiling, baking and chipping. A good all-round potato.

BINTJI
A waxy, oval potato with pale cream skin and pale yellow flesh. Good for boiling, roasting and salads. Available washed and unwashed.

NICOLA
A yellow-fleshed potato with creamy skin. This is a very good all-rounder which is suitable for boiling, baking and mashing.

TASMANIAN PINK EYE (Southern Gold)
A round waxy potato with cream skin with a mauve blush at one end. Good for boiling, mashing and in salads.

PONTIAC
A round potato with red skin, deep eyes and white flesh. An all-purpose potato, suitable for puréeing, grating, baking and boiling, but not chipping.

CHATS
Not a variety, but small washed potatoes go by this name.

Clockwise, from top left: Sebago, Kipfler, Spunta, Sweet potatoes, Sebago, Coliban, Bison, Jersey Royal, Pink Fir Apple

SEBAGO
An all-purpose white potato, the most common in Australia. It can be boiled, baked, fried or mashed and also used in salads.

KIPFLER
A waxy finger-shaped potato with creamy skin and yellow flesh. It has a nutty flavour and is most suitable for steaming and for use in salads and stews.

SPUNTA
A large potato with creamy coloured skin and floury, yellow flesh. It mashes very well and is good for frying and baking.

BISON
A round dark-red potato with shallow eyes and white flesh that is easy to peel. An all-purpose potato, good for boiling, baking and mashing.

COLIBAN
A round, white, smooth-skinned potato which is always sold washed. It is good for baking and boiling as well as mashing.

JERSEY ROYAL
A true new potato with creamy yellow skin that rubs off easily, a creamy flesh and delicate flavour. It is best served whole as the flesh is quite tender. Suitable for boiling and steaming, very good in salads and equally delicious served hot or cold.

PINK FIR APPLE
A slightly elongated, knobbly tuber, which is easier to peel after cooking, though it is often eaten with the skin on. The flesh is pinkish yellow and the flavour nutty. The waxy texture is perfect for salads or whole in stews.

SWEET POTATO
Sweet potatoes, which are high in vitamins A and C, may have buff, red or purple skins, but they all have sweet mealy flesh and a longish knobbly shape. There are two main varieties, one with a yellow/orange

flesh and dryer texture, the other with a white flesh and wetter texture. Although not true potatoes, they can be used in the same way and are often used as a substitute for potatoes. They can be roasted, boiled, fried or mashed and make good baking potatoes. Their flavour is enhanced by sweet spices such as cinnamon. Sweet potatoes are also known by the New Zealand Maori name of kumera.

SELECTING THE TYPE
Floury potatoes have a low moisture and sugar content and lots of starch. They bake and mash very well, make crisp golden chips and roast potatoes and are good for gnocchi and breads.

Waxy potatoes have a high moisture content and are low in starch. They hold their shape well when boiled and steamed. They are good in salads and stews, grate and slice well, but do not make particularly good chips or mash. **Salad** potatoes and new potatoes tend to be waxy and have a distinct flavour. They should not be peeled.

NUTRITION
Potatoes are an important source of complex carbohydrates and minerals, contain vitamins C and B6 and are low in sodium, high in potassium. Contrary to popular belief, potatoes do not add to the waistline if prepared simply, without fatty additions.

BUYING AND STORING
Potatoes should be firm to the touch, and not wrinkled, cracked, sprouting or green. They will keep best if removed from their plastic bag and stored away from light in a cool, well-ventilated place. If exposed to light, potatoes develop a green tinge. This part can be toxic and should not be eaten. If potatoes are stored in the refrigerator, they become sweeter than if stored at room temperature. Unwashed potatoes keep better as the layer of earth protects them. Older potatoes keep for a couple of weeks, whereas new potatoes are better eaten soon after purchase and should be bought in smaller quantities.

POTATO CLASSICS

CREAMY POTATO GRATIN

Preparation time: 20 minutes
Total cooking time: 40 minutes
Serves 4–6

750 g (1½ lb) potatoes
1 onion
1 cup (125 g/4 oz) grated
　　Cheddar cheese
1½ cups (375 ml/12 fl oz)
　　cream
2 teaspoons chicken stock
　　powder

1 Preheat the oven to moderate 180°C (350°F/Gas 4). Peel the potatoes and thinly slice them. Peel the onion and slice it into rings.
2 Arrange a layer of overlapping potato slices in a baking dish and top with a layer of onion rings. Divide the cheese in half and set aside one half to use as a topping. Sprinkle a little of the remaining cheese over the onion. Continue layering in this order until all the potato and the onion have been used, finishing with a little of the grated cheese.

3 Pour the cream into a small jug, add the chicken stock powder and whisk gently until thoroughly combined. Pour the mixture over the layered potato and onion and sprinkle the top with the reserved grated cheese. Bake for 40 minutes, or until the potato is tender, the cheese has melted and the top is golden brown.

NUTRITION PER SERVE (6)
Protein 9 g; Fat 35 g; Carbohydrate 15 g; Dietary Fibre 2 g; Cholesterol 100 mg; 1635 kJ (390 cal)

COOK'S FILE

Notes: A gratin is any dish topped with cheese and/or breadcrumbs and cooked until browned. There are many versions of potato gratin. Some are creamy like this one, others less so. Gratin dauphinois is one of the better known potato dishes.

If you prefer, you can use different types of stock, including vegetable, to vary the flavour.

Waxy or all-purpose potatoes are best as they hold their shape better when slow-cooked in this way.

If you have a mandolin, use it to cut the potatoes into thin slices. If not, make sure you use a very sharp knife. Peel the skin very thinly.

Sprinkle a little of the grated cheese over each layer.

Pour the cream mixture over the potato and onion.

POTATO SALAD

Preparation time: 40 minutes
Total cooking time: 5 minutes
Serves 4

600 g (1 1/4 lb) waxy or salad
    potatoes
1 small onion, finely chopped
2–3 celery sticks, thinly sliced
1 small green capsicum,
    chopped
2 tablespoons finely chopped
    parsley

Dressing
3/4 cup (185 g/6 oz) mayonnaise
1–2 tablespoons vinegar or
    lemon juice
2 tablespoons sour cream

1 Wash the potatoes thoroughly, peeling them if you prefer, and cut into bite-sized pieces. Cook in a large pan of boiling water for 5 minutes, or until just tender (pierce several pieces with a small sharp knife—the knife should come away easily). Drain, transfer to a bowl and cool completely.
2 Mix together the onion, celery, capsicum and half the chopped parsley and add to the cooled potato.
3 To make the dressing, mix together the mayonnaise, vinegar and sour cream, and season with salt and pepper, to taste. If you prefer a thinner dressing, add a little more vinegar or juice. Pour over the salad and gently toss to combine, being careful not to break up the pieces of potato. Can be garnished with the remaining parsley.

NUTRITION PER SERVE
Protein 5 g; Fat 20 g; Carbohydrate 30 g;
Dietary Fibre 4 g; Cholesterol 30 mg;
1340 kJ (320 cal)

If a sharp knife comes away easily when inserted, the potato is done.

Add the combined onion, celery, capsicum and parsley to the cooled potato.

Pour the thoroughly combined dressing over the potato and toss gently.

INDIVIDUAL OVEN-BAKED ROSTI

Preparation time: 20–25 minutes
Total cooking time: 55 minutes
Makes 12

500 g (1 lb) waxy potatoes, peeled
1 medium onion
30 g (1 oz) butter, melted

1 Preheat the oven to hot 220°C (425°F/Gas 7). Cook the potatoes in a pan of boiling salted water for 7 minutes, or until just tender. Drain.
2 Prepare a 12-hole muffin tin, with holes measuring 6 cm (2½ inches) at the top and 4.5 cm (1¾ inches) at the base, by brushing with a little of the butter. Grate the potatoes and onion, mix together in a bowl and pour the melted butter over the mixture. Season with salt and mix together well. Using two forks, divide the mixture among the muffin holes, gently pressing it in. Cook the rosti in the oven for 45 minutes, or until cooked through and golden.
3 Using a small palette knife, loosen each rosti around the edge and lift out. Serve on a warm serving dish.

NUTRITION PER ROSTI
Protein 1 g; Fat 2 g; Carbohydrate 6 g; Dietary Fibre 1 g; Cholesterol 6 mg; 200 kJ (50 cal)

Lightly brush the muffin tin with some of the melted butter.

Use two forks to put some mixture in each hole.

Before lifting the rosti out, loosen around the edge with a small palette knife.

HASH BROWNS

Preparation time: 30 minutes
Total cooking time: 15–20 minutes
Serves 4

**800 g (1 lb 10 oz) waxy
   potatoes, peeled
120 g (4 oz) butter**

1 Boil or steam the potatoes until just tender. Drain, cool, chop coarsely and season with salt and pepper.

2 Heat half the butter in a large heavy-based frying pan and put four lightly greased egg rings in it. Spoon the potato evenly into the egg rings, filling the rings to the top and pressing the potato down lightly to form flat cakes. Cook over medium-low heat for 5–7 minutes, or until a crust forms on the bottom. Be careful not to burn. Shake the pan gently to prevent sticking.

3 Turn the hash browns with a large spatula. Gently loosen the egg rings and remove with tongs. Cook for another 4–5 minutes, or until browned and crisp. Remove from the pan and drain on paper towels. Add a little more butter to the pan, if necessary, and cook the remaining potato in the same way. Serve immediately.

NUTRITION PER SERVE
Protein 3 g; Fat 25 g; Carbohydrate 35 g; Dietary Fibre 4 g; Cholesterol 75 mg; 1535 kJ (365 cal)

COOK'S FILE

Note: If you don't have egg rings, cook as one large cake.

Fill the egg rings with the chopped potato and press the mixture down lightly.

Cook until a crust forms on the bottom. Be careful to prevent burning or sticking.

Use a large spatula to turn the hash browns over.

BUBBLE AND SQUEAK

Preparation time: 25–30 minutes
Total cooking time: 20 minutes
Serves 4

500 g (1 lb) cold mashed or
  chopped cooked potato
500 g (1 lb) mixture of chopped
  cooked vegetables, such as
  cabbage, carrots, Brussels
  sprouts, parsnip, celery
  or beans

1 cup (150 g/5 oz) cooked meat
  or sausage, diced
60 g (2 oz) butter
1 teaspoon white wine vinegar

1 Mix the potato, vegetables and meat in a bowl. Heat the butter in a heavy-based frying pan, add the mixture and cook over medium-high heat for 5 minutes, turning frequently.
2 Flatten and press the mixture in the pan and cook for 5–10 minutes, or until golden and crisp on the base. Turn large portions of mixture and

cook for another 5–6 minutes, or until the underside is golden. Sprinkle with vinegar and season, to taste.

NUTRITION PER SERVE
Protein 110 g; Fat 20 g; Carbohydrate 25 g; Dietary Fibre 7 g; Cholesterol 55 mg; 1380 kJ (330 cal)

COOK'S FILE

Note: Traditionally, day-old, cooked vegetables are used, with mashed potato and cabbage forming the base, but mashed or chopped pumpkin and sweet potato are also delicious.

Mix together the cold potato, mixed vegetables and cooked meat.

Press the mixture down firmly in the pan so it forms a crispy base.

Use a spatula to turn over portions of the mixture, so it browns on both sides.

POTATO GNOCCHI WITH TOMATO SAUCE

Preparation time: 1 hour
Total cooking time: 45 minutes
Serves 4

500 g (1 lb) floury potatoes,
   unpeeled
1 egg yolk
3 tablespoons freshly grated
   Parmesan
1 cup (125 g/4 oz) plain flour

Tomato sauce
425 g (14 oz) can tomatoes
1 small onion, chopped
1 celery stick, chopped
1 small carrot, chopped
1 tablespoon shredded basil
1 teaspoon chopped thyme
1 clove garlic, crushed
1 teaspoon caster sugar

1 Steam or boil the potatoes until just tender. Drain thoroughly and allow to cool for 10 minutes before peeling and mashing them.
2 Measure 2 cups of the mashed potato into a large bowl, mix in the egg yolk, Parmesan, 1/4 teaspoon of salt and some freshly ground black pepper. Gradually add flour, using enough to form a slightly sticky dough. Knead for 5 minutes, adding more flour if necessary, until a smooth dough is formed.
3 Divide the dough into four portions and roll each portion on a lightly floured surface to form a sausage shape, about 2 cm (3/4 inch) thick.
4 Cut the rolls into 2.5 cm (1 inch) slices and shape each piece into an oval. Press each oval into the palm of your hand against a floured fork, to

flatten slightly and indent one side with a pattern. As you make the gnocchi place them in a single layer on a baking tray and cover until ready to use.
5 To make the tomato sauce, mix all the ingredients with salt and pepper in a medium pan. Bring to the boil, reduce the heat to medium-low and simmer for 30 minutes, stirring occasionally. Allow to cool, then process in a food processor or blender, until smooth. Reheat if necessary, just before serving.
6 Cook the gnocchi, in batches, in a large pan of boiling salted water, uncovered, for 2 minutes, or until the gnocchi float to the surface. Drain well. Serve the gnocchi tossed through the sauce. Garnish with Parmesan shavings and basil leaves if you wish.

NUTRITION PER SERVE
Protein 10 g; Fat 4 g; Carbohydrate 45 g; Dietary Fibre 5 g; Cholesterol 50 mg; 1125 kJ (270 cal)

COOK'S FILE

Notes: The gnocchi can be prepared several hours in advance and arranged on a tray in a single layer to prevent them sticking together. Cover and keep refrigerated.
   Gnocchi was traditionally made using potatoes baked in their skins. This results in a drier dough that is easy to work with, so if you have time you can use this method.
Variation: Put the cooked gnocchi in a well-greased serving dish, dot with butter, sprinkle with 1 cup (120 g/ 4 oz) of grated fontina or Cheddar cheese and 1/2 cup (50 g/13/4 oz) of freshly grated Parmesan. Bake for 10 minutes in a very hot 240°C (475°F/ Gas 9) oven, or until the cheese is golden brown.

Slowly add flour to the potato mixture, until a slightly sticky dough is formed.

Knead the dough for about 5 minutes or until smooth, adding flour if necessary.

Roll each portion into a sausage shape, on a lightly floured surface.

Press each oval with a floured fork to flatten slightly and make an indentation.

Put all the ingredients for the sauce in a pan and season with salt and pepper.

Cook the gnocchi in a large pan of boiling water until they float to the surface.

POTATO SCALLOPS

Preparation time: 40 minutes
Total cooking time: 15–20 minutes
Serves 4–6

**3–4 medium potatoes, peeled
and thinly sliced
1 cup (125 g/4 oz) self-raising
flour
¹/₄ cup (30 g/1 oz) cornflour
1 teaspoon lemon juice
1 tablespoon oil
plain flour, for coating
oil, for deep-frying**

1 Pat the potatoes dry with paper towels. Sift the self-raising flour, cornflour and some salt and pepper into a bowl. Make a well in the centre, slowly whisk in ³/₄ cup (185 ml/6 fl oz) water and mix to a smooth paste. Add another 3 tablespoons water with the lemon juice and 1 tablespoon oil.
2 Coat the potato slices lightly with plain flour and shake off any excess. Dip each slice into the batter, coat well and drain the excess before frying.
3 Half fill a deep, heavy-based pan with oil and heat to 160°C/315°F (a cube of bread dropped in the oil will brown in 30 seconds). Deep-fry the potato scallops, a few at a time, until lightly golden. Drain on paper towels. When all the scallops have been fried, increase the oil temperature slightly, to 180°C/350°F (a cube of bread dropped into the oil will brown in 15 seconds), add the scallops again and fry for another 1–2 minutes, or until golden brown. Drain on paper towels and serve immediately. Scallops are delicious served with salt and lemon wedges.

NUTRITION PER SERVE (6)
Protein 3 g; Fat 13 g; Carbohydrate 35 g;
Dietary Fibre 2 g; Cholesterol 0 mg;
740 kJ (175 cal)

Slowly whisk in the water to make a smooth paste.

Coat the scallops lightly in plain flour, then dip in the batter.

Deep-fry the scallops in hot oil in batches, until lightly golden.

POTATO CROQUETTES

Preparation time: 45 minutes
+ refrigeration
Total cooking time: 5–10 minutes
Makes 12

**750 g (1¹/₂ lb) floury potatoes,
 peeled and chopped
2 tablespoons cream or melted
 butter
3 eggs, lightly beaten
¹/₄ teaspoon nutmeg
plain flour, for coating**

**1¹/₂ cups (150 g/5 oz) dry
 breadcrumbs
oil, for deep-frying**

1 Boil the potato in salted water until tender, drain and mash. Stir in the cream or butter, one-third of the beaten egg, nutmeg and some salt and pepper. Spread onto a plate. cover and refrigerate for at least 30 minutes.

2 Divide the mixture into 12 even-sized portions and form each into a sausage shape about 8 cm (3 inches) long. Roll the croquettes in flour and shake off the excess. Dip in the remaining egg, coat evenly in the breadcrumbs and then shake off the excess. Cover and refrigerate for at least 2 hours.

3 Half fill a deep heavy-based pan with oil and heat to 180°C/350°F (a cube of bread dropped in the oil will brown in 15 seconds). Cook the croquettes in batches for 5 minutes, or until golden. Remove carefully, drain on paper towels and keep warm.

NUTRITION PER CROQUETTE
Protein 5 g; Fat 7 g; Carbohydrate 25 g;
Dietary Fibre 2 g; Cholesterol 50 mg;
715 kJ (170 cal)

Divide the chilled mixture into twelve portions and roll into croquettes.

Coat the croquettes in plain flour, then egg, then breadcrumbs.

Lower the croquettes into the hot oil and deep-fry, a few at a time.

POTATOES WITH SPICY TOMATO SAUCE

Preparation time: 25 minutes
Total cooking time: 50 minutes
Serves 4

2 kg (4 lb) chats or baby potatoes
4 tablespoons olive oil
1 tablespoon chopped rosemary
2 onions, chopped
3 cloves garlic, chopped
1 teaspoon chopped red chilli
1/2 cup (125 g/4 oz) tomato paste
1 kg (2 lb) Roma tomatoes,
    chopped

1/2 cup (125 ml/4 fl oz) red wine
1 tablespoon balsamic vinegar
1 teaspoon soft brown sugar
1/4 cup (15 g/1/2 oz) chopped
    parsley

1 Preheat the oven to moderate 180°C (350°F/Gas 4). Put the potatoes in a baking dish, drizzle with half of the oil and sprinkle with the rosemary and 1 teaspoon each of salt and pepper. Bake for 50 minutes, shaking the dish regularly, or until the potatoes are brown and crisp.
2 While the potatoes are baking, make the sauce. Heat the remaining oil in a large heavy-based pan. Add the onion, garlic and chilli; cook for 5 minutes over medium heat. Add the tomato paste and cook for 3 minutes, stirring regularly. If the mixture becomes too dry, add a little water. Add 2 cups (500 ml/16 fl oz) of water with the tomato, wine, vinegar and sugar. Bring to the boil, stirring. Reduce the heat and simmer for 25 minutes, or until thick. Season, to taste, and stir in the parsley.
3 Divide the potatoes among serving bowls and pour the sauce over the top.

NUTRITION PER SERVE
Protein 15 g; Fat 20 g; Carbohydrate 80 g; Dietary Fibre 15 g; Cholesterol 0 mg; 2505 kJ (600 cal)

Sprinkle the roughly chopped fresh rosemary over the oiled potatoes.

Bake the potatoes until they are lightly browned and turning crisp.

When the sauce has thickened, add the parsley and stir through.

Pour the clarified butter out of the pan, leaving the white sediment behind.

Use a very sharp knife to thinly slice the peeled potatoes.

Overlap the potatoes in a spiral pattern on the bottom of the pan or dish.

After 20 minutes, remove the foil or lid and cook, uncovered, until tender.

POTATOES ANNA

Preparation time: 30 minutes
Total cooking time: 1 hour 5 minutes
Serves 4

1 kg (2 lb) potatoes, peeled
90 g (3 oz) clarified butter
(see note) or ghee

1 Preheat the oven to moderately hot 200°C (400°F/Gas 6). Slice the potatoes thinly. Melt the clarified butter and use a little to grease the sides of an ovenproof frying pan or shallow flameproof dish, about 25 cm (10 inches) diameter and 5 cm (2 inches) deep.

2 Dry the potato on paper towels and arrange a layer in the bottom of the pan, overlapping neatly in a spiral pattern. Pour 20 g (³/4 oz) of clarified butter onto each layer and season with salt and seasoned pepper. Build up three to four layers, then pour the remaining clarified butter over the top, cover with a lid or a double layer of foil and bake in the oven for 20 minutes.

3 Remove the lid or foil and cook, uncovered, for 30–40 minutes or until the potato is very tender and the top is golden and crisp. Pour off any excess butter. Loosen the sides with a spatula and serve from the pan or, if preferred, invert onto a serving plate to serve immediately, cut into wedges.

NUTRITION PER SERVE
Protein 6 g; Fat 40 g; Carbohydrate 35 g; Dietary Fibre 4 g; Cholesterol 125 mg; 2200 kJ (525 cal)

COOK'S FILE

Note: Clarified butter is used because it will cook at a higher temperature without burning. To clarify butter, heat butter over low heat in a small pan for 5 minutes but do not allow it to brown. Turn off the heat and leave to settle for 5 minutes. Remove the scum from the top with a slotted spoon. Pour off the butter, leaving white sediment behind. Use melted.

DUCHESS POTATOES

Preparation time: 20 minutes
+ refrigeration
Total cooking time: 45 minutes
Serves 6

**860 g (1 lb 12 oz) floury
potatoes, peeled and
quartered
2 eggs, plus 1 extra yolk
¼ cup (60 ml/2 fl oz) cream
2 tablespoons freshly grated
Parmesan
¼ teaspoon grated nutmeg**

1 Boil or steam the potato until just tender, then drain and return to the pan. Turn the heat to very low and shake the pan for 1–2 minutes to dry out the potato. Transfer the potato to a bowl and mash.
2 Beat together the 2 eggs, cream, Parmesan, nutmeg and some salt and freshly ground black pepper. Add to the potato and mash until smooth. Cover and refrigerate for about 40 minutes, until cold. Preheat the oven to moderate 180°C (350°F/Gas 4).
3 Put the potato mixture in a piping bag with a 1.5 cm (⅝ inch) star nozzle. Pipe the mixture in swirls, not too

close together, onto greased oven trays. Brush lightly with the extra egg yolk, to give a golden, crisp finish. Bake for 15–20 minutes, or until golden. Serve hot, perhaps garnished with a little paprika.

NUTRITION PER SERVE
Protein 7 g; Fat 8 g; Carbohydrate 20 g;
Dietary Fibre 2 g; Cholesterol 105 mg;
755 kJ (180 cal)

COOK'S FILE

Note: Duchess potatoes can be prepared in advance and refrigerated. Just before serving, brush with egg yolk and bake as per the recipe instructions.

Shake the potatoes in the pan over very low heat, to dry them out.

Add the egg and cream mixture to the potato and mash until smooth.

Pipe the mixture in swirls, not too close together, onto greased oven trays.

HASSELBACK POTATOES

Preparation time: 20 minutes
Total cooking time: 45 minutes
Serves 4

**60 g (2 oz) butter, melted
4 medium potatoes
2 tablespoons fresh white
breadcrumbs
3 tablespoons grated Parmesan
½ teaspoon paprika**

1 Preheat the oven to moderately hot 200°C (400°F/Gas 6). Brush a shallow baking tray with just a little of the melted butter.
2 Peel the potatoes and cut each one into two even-sized pieces. Put each potato, cut-side-down, on a board. Make thin evenly-spaced cuts about two-thirds of the way through, then place, flat-side-down, on the tray. Brush liberally with melted butter. Bake them for 30 minutes, brushing occasionally with butter.
3 Combine the breadcrumbs and

Parmesan and sprinkle evenly over the potato. Sprinkle with the paprika and bake the potato for another 15 minutes, or until golden brown. Serve immediately.

NUTRITION PER SERVE
Protein 6 g; Fat 15 g; Carbohydrate 20 g;
Dietary Fibre 2 g; Cholesterol 45 mg;
955 kJ (230 cal)

COOK'S FILE

Note: For even cooking, choose potatoes of a similar size. Use Cheddar instead of Parmesan, if preferred.

Make evenly-spaced cuts about two-thirds of the way through each potato.

Brush the potatoes with melted butter during cooking.

Sprinkle the combined breadcrumbs and Parmesan over the potatoes.

*Duchess potatoes (top)
with Hasselback potatoes*

Perfect chips

The best potatoes to use to make perfect potato chips are floury varieties such as Spunta or King Edward. Fry them twice to achieve a golden crispy outside and light fluffy middle.

THE PERFECT CHIP

Peel 6 large potatoes, wash and pat dry. Cut lengthways into 1 cm (1/2 inch) wide slices and then into 1 cm (1/2 inch) wide chips. Put them in a bowl of iced water as you cut them. Drain and dry thoroughly. To deep-fry safely, the temperature of the oil must be controlled, preferably in a deep-fryer, using a thermometer. If using a pan, it must be a heavy-bottomed one, filled no more than half full, as the level will rise as the chips give off water. For the first frying, heat the oil to 160°C/315°F. Test by dropping a cube of bread into the oil—it will brown in 30 seconds when ready. If it browns in less than 10 seconds, the oil is far too hot, so lower the heat. Cook the chips, in batches, for 4–5 minutes, or until pale golden. Drain on paper towels. Before serving, reheat the oil to 180°C/350°F (a cube of bread will brown in 15 seconds) and cook for 2–3 minutes, until golden and crisp. Drain and sprinkle with salt. Serves 2–4.

NUTRITION PER SERVE (4)
Protein 9 g; Fat 15 g; Carbohydrate 50 g; Dietary Fibre 6 g; Cholesterol 0 mg; 1550 kJ (370 cal)

FRENCH FRIES

Prepare the potatoes as described in The Perfect Chip, cutting into 5 mm (1/4 inch) thick slices and 5 mm (1/4 inch) wide sticks. Half fill a heavy-based pan with oil and heat to 180°C/350°F. Cook the French fries, in batches, for 5–10 minutes, or until golden and crisp. Drain thoroughly on paper towels and sprinkle with salt. Serve with tomato sauce or mustard mayonnaise. Serves 2–4.

NUTRITION PER SERVE (4)
Protein 9 g; Fat 20 g; Carbohydrate 50 g; Dietary Fibre 6 g; Cholesterol 0 mg; 1725 kJ (415 cal)

POTATO RIBBONS

Peel 6 large potatoes, wash and pat dry with paper towels. Using a vegetable peeler, peel the potato into ribbons. Half fill a heavy-based pan with oil and heat to 180°C/350°F. Cook, in batches, for 3–4 minutes, or until crisp and golden. Drain on paper towels. Season and drizzle with sweet Thai chilli sauce. Serves 4–6.

NUTRITION PER SERVE (6)
Protein 9 g; Fat 25 g; Carbohydrate 50 g; Dietary Fibre 6 g; Cholesterol 0 mg; 1900 kJ (455 cal)

BAKED ROSEMARY POTATO CHIPS

Preheat the oven to hot 220°C (425°C/Gas 7). Scrub 6 large potatoes and pat them dry with paper towels. Cut each potato into about ten wedges and put them in a bowl. In a small bowl, mix 2 tablespoons of olive oil, a crushed clove of garlic, 1 tablespoon of chopped rosemary and some salt and freshly ground black pepper. Stir the mixture into the wedges and spread the wedges in a shallow baking dish in a single layer. Bake for about 45–50 minutes, until golden, turning occasionally. Drain off any excess oil and serve. Serves 2–4.

NUTRITION PER SERVE (4)
Protein 9 g; Fat 10 g; Carbohydrate 50 g; Dietary Fibre 6 g; Cholesterol 0 mg; 1395 kJ (330 cal)

SHOESTRINGS

Prepare the potatoes as described in The Perfect Chip, cutting them into 3 mm (1/8 inch) thick slices and 3 mm (1/8 inch) wide sticks. Use a mandolin if you have one. Half fill a heavy-based pan with oil and heat to 180°C/350°F.

Cook the shoestrings, in batches, for 5–10 minutes or until golden brown and crisp. Drain thoroughly on paper towels and sprinkle with salt. Serve with tomato sauce or mustard mayonnaise. Serves 2–4.

NUTRITION PER SERVE (4)
Protein 9 g; Fat 25 g; Carbohydrate 50 g; Dietary Fibre 6 g; Cholesterol 0 mg; 1900 kJ (455 cal)

BAKED POTATO WEDGES WITH PARMESAN

Scrub 6 large potatoes and cut each into about ten wedges and soak in cold water for 10 minutes. Preheat the oven to hot 220°C (425°C/Gas 7). Drain the wedges and dry on paper towels. Toss the wedges in 2 tablespoons of olive oil and tip them into a shallow baking dish in a single layer. Bake for 45–50 minutes, until golden and crisp, turning occasionally. Drain on paper towels and sprinkle with salt, pepper and finely grated Parmesan, to taste. Serves 2–4.

NUTRITION PER SERVE (4)
Protein 15 g; Fat 15 g; Carbohydrate 50 g; Dietary Fibre 6 g; Cholesterol 14 mg; 1650 kJ (395 cal)

CHILLI POTATO SKINS

Scrub 6 large potatoes and pat dry with paper towels; prick each potato twice with a fork. Preheat the oven to hot 210°C (415°C/Gas 6–7) and bake the potatoes for 1 hour, turning once, until the skins are crisp and the flesh is soft. Remove from the oven and cool. Halve the potatoes and scoop out the flesh, leaving 5 mm (1/4 inch) of the potato in the skin. Cut each half into three wedges. Half fill a heavy-based pan with oil and heat to 180°C/350°F. Cook the potato skins, in batches, for 2–3 minutes, or until crisp. Drain on paper towels and sprinkle with salt, pepper and chilli powder or hot paprika. Serve with a cucumber and yoghurt dip. Serves 4–6.

NUTRITION PER SERVE (6)
Protein 5 g; Fat 20 g; Carbohydrate 45 g; Dietary Fibre 4 g; Cholesterol 0 mg; 1550 kJ (370 cal)

Left to right: Perfect chips, French fries, Potato ribbons, Baked rosemary potato chips, Shoestrings, Baked potato wedges with Parmesan, Chilli potato skins

ROAST POTATOES WITH ROSEMARY

Preparation time: 15 minutes
Total cooking time: 30 minutes
Serves 4

750 g (1½ lb) Pink Fir Apple potatoes, unpeeled
1½ tablespoons olive oil

8 large cloves garlic, unpeeled
2 tablespoons rosemary leaves

1 Preheat the oven to hot 200°C (400°F/Gas 6). Cut the potatoes in half lengthways and pat dry. Heat the oil in a large oven dish, add the potato and garlic and toss for a minute to coat in the hot oil. Remove from the heat and turn all the potato cut-side-up. Sprinkle with rosemary.

2 Bake for 30 minutes, or until cooked and golden. The garlic will be creamy and soft. Serve immediately.

NUTRITION PER SERVE
Protein 5 g; Fat 7 g; Carbohydrate 25 g; Dietary Fibre 4 g; Cholesterol 0 mg; 800 kJ (190 cal)

COOK'S FILE

Variation: Use Kipfler potatoes instead of Pink Fir Apple, if preferred.

Scrub the potatoes well and cut in half lengthways. Pat dry.

Toss the potatoes in the hot oil and then arrange cut-side-up.

Sprinkle fresh rosemary leaves over the potatoes before baking.

POTATOES WITH GARLIC MAYONNAISE

Preparation time: 30 minutes
Total cooking time: 1 hour 30 minutes
Serves 4–6

9–12 cloves garlic, unpeeled
3/4 cup (185 ml/6 fl oz) extra
    virgin olive oil
1.5 kg (3 lb) potatoes, unpeeled,
    cut into chunks
1 tablespoon chopped thyme
2 teaspoons each chopped
    rosemary and oregano leaves
2 egg yolks
2 tablespoons lemon juice

1 Preheat the oven to moderate 180°C (350°F/Gas 4). Pierce the garlic cloves in a few places, put them in a baking dish and drizzle 3 tablespoons of the olive oil over them. Cook for 25–30 minutes, or until tender. Turn the garlic a few times and check it doesn't overcook or it will become hard and bitter. Remove from the dish and leave to cool slightly.

2 Pour the oil from roasting the garlic into a large baking dish. Increase the oven to hot 210°C (415°F/ Gas 6–7) and heat the oil in the dish. Add the potato and herbs and toss in the oil. Season with salt and pepper and roast for 1 hour, or until crisp and golden, turning two or three times.

3 Peel the garlic cloves and mash with a fork. Put the egg yolks in a food processor and, with the motor running, add the remaining oil in a thin stream, until the mixture is thick. Add the garlic and process to combine. Mix in the lemon juice and season with pepper. Serve the garlic mayonnaise with the potatoes.

NUTRITION PER SERVE (6)
Protein 7 g; Fat 30 g; Carbohydrate 35 g; Dietary Fibre 5 g; Cholesterol 60 mg; 1870 kJ (445 cal)

COOK'S FILE

Note: It may seem to be a lot of garlic but roasted garlic becomes creamy and has a mellow flavour.

Drizzle some of the oil over the garlic cloves in the dish.

Add the potatoes and herbs to the hot oil and toss well.

Mash the roasted garlic with a fork before adding to the mayonnaise.

POTATO PIES

Preparation time: 25 minutes
Total cooking time: 55 minutes
Makes 6

1 tablespoon oil
1 onion, finely chopped
1 clove garlic, crushed
500 g (1 lb) beef mince
2 tablespoons plain flour
2 cups (500 ml/16 fl oz) beef
    stock
2 tablespoons tomato paste
1 tablespoon Worcestershire
    sauce
6 sheets frozen shortcrust
    pastry, thawed
45 g (1½ oz) butter
¼ cup (60 ml/2 fl oz) milk
1 kg (2 lb) floury potatoes,
    cooked and mashed

1 Preheat the oven to hot 210°C (415°F/gas 6–7). Heat the oil in a pan, add the onion and cook for 5 minutes, or until soft. Add the garlic and cook for another minute. Add the mince and cook over medium heat for 5 minutes, or until browned, breaking up any lumps with a fork.

2 Sprinkle the flour over the meat and stir to combine. Add the stock, tomato paste, sauce and salt and pepper to the pan; stir for 2 minutes. Bring to the boil, then reduce the heat slightly and simmer for 5 minutes, or until the mixture has reduced and thickened. Allow to cool completely.

3 Brush six 11 cm (4½ inch) pie tins with melted butter or oil. Using a plate as a guide, cut the pastry into 15 cm (6 inch) circles and line the pie tins. Cut sheets of greaseproof paper to cover each tin, spread dried beans, rice or baking beads over the paper and bake for 7 minutes. Remove the paper and beads and cook the pastry for another 5 minutes. Allow to cool.

4 Spoon the meat filling into the pastry cases. Stir the butter and milk into the mashed potato and pipe or spread over the top of the meat mixture. Bake for 20 minutes, or until lightly golden.

NUTRITION PER PIE
Protein 35 g; Fat 65 g; Carbohydrate 100 g; Dietary Fibre 6 g; Cholesterol 130 mg; 4730 kJ (1130 cal)

Line the pie tins with the circles of pastry, pressing gently to fit.

Line the pastry with greaseproof paper and cover with baking beads or rice.

Spoon the meat filling into the blind-baked pastry cases.

Pipe the potato over the meat filling, or spread roughly with a fork.

POTATO SALAD WITH MUSTARD AND HONEY

Preparation time:15 minutes
Total cooking time: 35 minutes
Serves 4–6

1 kg (2 lb) baby red potatoes, unpeeled
4 slices prosciutto
4 spring onions

Mustard and honey dressing
2 tablespoons white wine vinegar
2 tablespoon honey
1 tablespoon wholegrain mustard
1/3 cup (80 ml/2³/4 fl oz) olive oil

1 Cut any larger potatoes in half, then cook until tender. Drain and cool.
2 Put the prosciutto on a baking tray and grill until crispy. Cool and break into pieces. Thinly slice the spring onion on the diagonal. Mix together the potato, prosciutto and spring onion in a bowl.
3 To make the mustard and honey dressing, put all the ingredients in a screw top jar and shake until well mixed. Pour over the potato salad.

NUTRITION PER SERVE (6)
Protein 7 g; Fat 15 g; Carbohydrate 30 g; Dietary Fibre 3 g; Cholesterol 8 mg; 1140 kJ (270 cal)

Check the potatoes with the point of a knife to make sure they are tender.

Place the prosciutto slices on a baking tray and grill until crisp.

With a sharp knife, thinly slice the spring onions on the diagonal.

DRY POTATO AND PEA CURRY

Preparation time: 15 minutes
Total cooking time: 30–35 minutes
Serves 4

750 g (1¹/2 lb) potatoes, peeled
2 teaspoons brown mustard
   seeds
2 tablespoons ghee or oil
2 cloves garlic, crushed
2 teaspoons grated fresh ginger
2 onions, sliced

1 teaspoon turmeric
¹/2 teaspoon chilli powder
1 teaspoon ground cumin
1 teaspoon garam masala
²/3 cup (100 g/3¹/2 oz) fresh or
   frozen peas
2 tablespoons chopped mint

1 Cut the potatoes into small cubes. Heat the mustard seeds in a dry pan until they start to pop. Add the ghee, garlic, ginger and onion to the pan and cook until soft. Add the potato, turmeric, chilli and cumin and season with salt and pepper.

2 Stir until the potatoes are coated with the spices. Add ¹/2 cup (125 ml/4 fl oz) of water to the pan, bring to the boil, reduce the heat and simmer, covered, for 15–20 minutes, or until tender, stirring occasionally.

3 Stir in the garam masala and peas and simmer, covered, for 3–5 minutes, or until the potato is cooked and the liquid absorbed. Stir in the mint. Serve with Indian breads, such as naan.

NUTRITION PER SERVE
Protein 7 g; Fat 3 g; Carbohydrate 30 g; Dietary Fibre 6 g; Cholesterol 0 mg; 725 kJ (175 cal)

Heat the mustard seeds in a dry pan until they begin to pop.

Add the ghee, garlic, ginger and onion to the pan and stir until soft.

Pour the water into the pan and, when boiling, lower the heat and simmer.

BACON AND ONION ROSTI CAKE

Preparation time: 30 minutes
  + 1 hour refrigeration
Total cooking time: 35–40 minutes
Serves 4

850 g (1 lb 12 oz) waxy
   potatoes, unpeeled and halved
60 g (2 oz) butter
6 thin bacon rashers, rind
   removed, chopped
1 small red onion, chopped

1–2 cloves garlic, crushed
2 tablespoons chopped parsley
1 teaspoon each chopped
   oregano and thyme leaves

1 Boil or steam the potato until just tender. Drain and refrigerate for 1 hour. Peel the potato, grate and put in a bowl.
2 Heat half the butter in a 23 cm (9 inch) heavy-based, non-stick pan. Add the bacon, onion and garlic and stir for 2 minutes, or until tender but not browned. Add to the potato. Add the herbs to the bowl and mix well.
3 Add a little butter to the pan, spread

the mixture into the pan and press with a spatula. Cook for 8 minutes or until a crust forms on the base. Shake the pan occasionally to stop the potato sticking.
4 Slide the rosti onto a greased flat plate, add the remaining butter to the pan and, when the butter has melted, flip the rosti carefully back into the pan on its uncooked side. Cook for 6 minutes, or until the base is crusty. Serve hot, cut into wedges.

NUTRITION PER SERVE
Protein 15 g; Fat 15 g; Carbohydrate 30 g; Dietary Fibre 4 g; Cholesterol 65 mg; 1385 kJ (330 cal)

Grate the peeled potatoes or, if you prefer, chop them coarsely.

Add the bacon, onion and garlic mixture to the potato.

Flip the rosti carefully back into the pan on its uncooked side.

Dry potato and pea curry (top) with Bacon and onion rosti cake

AROUND THE WORLD

CRISPY POTATO SKINS WITH GARLIC AND SESAME DIP

Preparation time: 35 minutes
Total cooking time: 1 hour 40 minutes
Serves 6 as a starter

900 g (1 lb 13 oz) potatoes,
  unpeeled
1 cup (80 g/2³/4 oz) fresh
  breadcrumbs
3 cloves garlic, crushed
3 tablespoons ground almonds
¹/3 cup (90 g/3 oz) mayonnaise
¹/3 cup (90 g/3 oz) thick natural
  yoghurt
1 tablespoon lemon juice
2 tablespoons chopped parsley
1 tablespoon chopped chives
3 tablespoons sesame seeds,
  roasted until golden
vegetable or olive oil, for
  shallow-frying
sticks of raw vegetables, for
  serving

1 Preheat the oven to moderately hot 200°C (400°F/Gas 6). Prick the potatoes with a sharp knife and bake on a baking tray for 1–1¹/2 hours, or until tender (cooking time will depend on the size of the potatoes).
2 Allow the potatoes to cool for a couple of minutes and cut each one in half lengthways. Using a spoon, scoop out most of the flesh into a bowl, leaving a thin layer of flesh in the potato skin. Cut each half of potato skin into three strips.
3 To make the dip, put 1 cup of the cooked potato flesh in a bowl, mash until smooth and allow to cool. (Leftover potato can be refrigerated for later use.) Add the breadcrumbs, crushed garlic, ground almonds, mayonnaise, yoghurt, lemon juice, parsley, chives and sesame seeds. Mix together well and season, to taste, with sea salt and black pepper. Transfer the dip to a serving bowl.
4 Heat the oil, about 5 cm (2 inches) deep, in a small pan, to 180°C/350°F (a cube of bread dropped into the oil will brown in 15 seconds). Fry the potato skins in batches, until crisp and golden. Keep them warm while cooking the remainder. Serve with the dip and sticks of raw vegetables.

NUTRITION PER SERVE
Protein 8 g; Fat 20 g; Carbohydrate 35 g; Dietary Fibre 4 g; Cholesterol 7 mg; 1495 kJ (355 cal)

Scoop out most of the potato, leaving a thin layer inside the skin.

Lower the potato skins, in batches, into hot oil and cook until crisp and golden.

POTATO PORCINI BAKE

Preparation time: 30 minutes
 + 15 minutes soaking
Total cooking time: 45 minutes
Serves 4–6

20 g (³/4 oz) dried porcini
 mushrooms
³/4 cup (185 ml/6 fl oz) hot milk
¹/2 cup (125 ml/4 fl oz) cream
1 kg (2 lb) waxy potatoes,
 unpeeled
30 g (1 oz) butter

1 clove garlic, crushed
¹/2 cup (60 g/2 oz) finely sliced
 spring onions
1 cup (120 g/4 oz) grated
 Fontina or Gruyère cheese

1 Lightly brush a large shallow ovenproof dish with oil. Make sure the porcini are free of dirt or grit and put them in a bowl with the hot milk. Cover the bowl and set aside for 15 minutes. Remove the porcini, finely chop them and then return to the milk. Add the cream.

2 Cut the potatoes into 1 cm (¹/2 inch)

slices and cook in boiling salted water until just tender, then drain well. Melt the butter in a small pan and cook the garlic and onion until soft.

3 Preheat the oven to moderate 180°C (350°F/Gas 4). Layer the potato in the dish with the spring onion and cheese, spooning the porcini mixture over each layer and seasoning with salt and pepper. Bake for 35 minutes, or until golden and tender. Serve hot.

NUTRITION PER SERVE (6)
Protein 10 g; Fat 20 g; Carbohydrate 25 g;
Dietary Fibre 3 g; Cholesterol 65 mg;
1375 kJ (330 cal)

Put the dried mushrooms in a bowl and leave to soak in the hot milk.

Cut the unpeeled potatoes into slices, then boil until tender.

Spoon the porcini mixture over each layer of potato.

POTATO AND CHICKEN THAI CURRY

Preparation time: 20 minutes
Total cooking time: 30 minutes
Serves 4–6

250 g (8 oz) chicken thigh fillets
250 g (8 oz) orange sweet
    potatoes, peeled
300 g (10 oz) potatoes, peeled
2 tablespoons oil
1 onion, chopped
1–2 tablespoons Thai yellow
    curry paste
1/4 teaspoon ground turmeric
1 2/3 cups (410 ml/13 fl oz)
    coconut milk
2 kaffir lime leaves
2 teaspoons fish sauce
2 teaspoons soft brown sugar
1 tablespoon lime juice
1 teaspoon lime rind
1/3 cup (10 g/1/4 oz) coriander
    leaves
1/3 cup (55 g/2 oz) roasted
    peanuts, roughly chopped

1 Remove the excess fat from the chicken and cut into bite-sized pieces. Cut the sweet potato and potato into bite-sized pieces. Heat the oil in a large heavy-based pan or wok and cook the onion until softened. Add the curry paste and turmeric and stir for 1 minute, or until aromatic.
2 Stir in the coconut milk and 1 cup (250 ml/8 fl oz) of water and bring to the boil. Reduce the heat and add the potato, sweet potato, chicken and kaffir lime leaves. Simmer for 15–20 minutes, or until the vegetables are tender and the chicken cooked through.
3 Add the fish sauce, sugar, lime juice and rind and stir to combine,

then add the coriander leaves. Garnish with the peanuts and serve with rice.

NUTRITION PER SERVE (6)
Protein 10 g; Fat 35 g; Carbohydrate 15 g; Dietary Fibre 3 g; Cholesterol 40 mg; 1805 kJ (430 cal)

COOK'S FILE

Note: Thai yellow curry paste is not as common as the red or green but is available from most Asian food stores. Kaffir lime leaves are now available in most supermarkets.

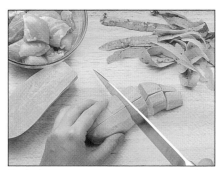

Peel the orange sweet potato and chop into bite-sized pieces.

When the onion has softened, stir in the curry paste and turmeric.

Reduce the heat and add the potato, sweet potato, chicken and lime leaves.

SPICY POTATO SALAD

Preparation time: 20 minutes
Total cooking time: 25 minutes
Serves 6

1 kg (2 lb) chats or baby
    potatoes, unpeeled
2 tablespoons vegetable oil
1 large onion, finely chopped
1 clove garlic, crushed
1 tablespoon finely chopped
    fresh ginger

1 teaspoon red curry paste
1 teaspoon garam masala
3 tablespoons lime juice
1 cup (155 g/5 oz) frozen baby
    peas
2 tablespoons chopped
    coriander
200 g (6¹/2 oz) thick continental-
    style yoghurt, for serving

1 Boil or steam the potatoes until just tender. Drain and allow to cool.
2 Heat the oil in a medium pan, add the onion, garlic and ginger and cook until the onion is soft but not brown. Add the curry paste and garam masala and cook over low heat, stirring constantly, for 3 minutes. Add the lime juice and mix well.
3 Cook the peas until tender, then drain. Cut the potatoes in half, then toss together with the warm onion mixture, peas and coriander. Serve with a spoonful of yoghurt.

NUTRITION PER SERVE
Protein 8 g; Fat 8 g; Carbohydrate 30 g; Dietary Fibre 5 g; Cholesterol 5 mg; 895 kJ (215 cal)

Boil the potatoes in their skins until tender. Test with the point of a knife.

Stir in the curry paste and garam masala and cook for 3 minutes.

Toss the potatoes with the warm onion mixture, peas and coriander.

POTATOES IN MEDITERRANEAN SAUCE

Preparation time: 30 minutes
Total cooking time: 50 minutes
Serves 4–6

1 kg (2 lb) chats or baby
   potatoes, unpeeled, halved
2 tablespoons olive oil
2 onions, finely chopped
3 cloves garlic, crushed
1 teaspoon sweet paprika
425 g (14 oz) can chopped
   tomatoes
2 tablespoons lemon juice

1/2 teaspoon grated lemon rind
2 teaspoons soft brown sugar
3 teaspoons tomato paste
1/2 teaspoon dried thyme
12 Kalamata olives
1 tablespoon capers, rinsed and
   roughly chopped
1 cup (140 g/4 1/2 oz) cubed feta
   cheese
1 tablespoon roughly chopped
   flat-leaf parsley

1 Boil the potato until just tender. Heat the olive oil in a large saucepan, add the onion and cook until soft and golden. Add the garlic and paprika and cook for another minute.

2 Stir in the tomato, lemon juice, lemon rind, sugar, tomato paste and thyme. Simmer, covered, for 5 minutes and then add the potato and toss to coat. Simmer, covered, for 20 minutes, or until the potato is cooked through. Stir occasionally to prevent burning.

3 Remove the pan from the heat and, just before serving, stir through the olives, capers and feta. Season with salt and freshly ground black pepper and scatter the parsley over the top. Serve immediately.

NUTRITION PER SERVE (6)
Protein 10 g; Fat 10 g; Carbohydrate 30 g; Dietary Fibre 5 g; Cholesterol 15 mg; 1120 kJ (270 cal)

Stir in the tomato, lemon juice and rind, sugar, tomato paste and thyme.

Add the potato to the tomato sauce and toss to coat.

Stir in the olives, capers and feta just before serving.

POTATO AND CORN FLATBREADS

Preparation time: 20 minutes
Total cooking time: 45 minutes
Serves 6

350 g (11 oz) floury potatoes,
    peeled and cubed
75 g (2½ oz) butter
1¼ cups (155 g/5 oz) plain
    flour
½ cup (75 g/2½ oz) fine yellow
    corn meal or polenta

4 teaspoons baking powder
½ teaspoon salt
75 ml (2½ fl oz) milk

1 Boil or steam the potato until tender, then mash until smooth. Stir in the butter, then add the flour, corn meal, baking powder and salt and mix well. Stir in the milk, a little at a time, until a loose dough forms (you may not need all the milk). Knead on a lightly floured surface for 20–25 strokes, to give a smooth dough. Preheat the oven to moderately hot 200°C (400°F/Gas 6).
2 Roll the dough out to a 25 cm

(10 inch) circle and cut into twelve wedges. Place, well-spaced, on a baking tray. Score a few lines across the top of each wedge and bake for 15–20 minutes, until golden. Delicious with soups and casseroles.

NUTRITION PER SERVE
Protein 6 g; Fat 10 g; Carbohydrate 35 g; Dietary Fibre 2 g; Cholesterol 35 mg; 1130 kJ (270 cal)

COOK'S FILE

Note: Best served immediately, but can be kept in an airtight container for up to three days. Reheat in the oven.

Stir enough of the milk into the mixture to form a loose dough.

Cut the circle of dough into twelve, even-sized wedges.

Score the top of each wedge to give a decorative finish.

POTATO AND FRENCH ONION SOUP

Preparation time: 25 minutes
Total cooking time: 1 hour 5 minutes
Serves 4–6

1 kg (2 lb) onions
60 g (2 oz) butter
3 cloves garlic, crushed
2 teaspoons soft brown sugar
1 tablespoon plain flour
1/2 cup (125 ml/4 fl oz) port

7 cups (1.75 litres) beef or
    vegetable stock
3 potatoes, unpeeled
1 tablespoon chopped parsley,
    for serving

1 Thinly slice the onions into rings. Heat the butter in a large heavy-based pan and add the onion and garlic. Cover the pan and sweat the onion over very low heat for 15–20 minutes, or until tender.
2 Add the sugar and cook, stirring occasionally, over medium heat for about 20 minutes, until caramelized. Stir in the flour and cook for another minute. Add the port and stock, bring to the boil, then reduce the heat and simmer for 15 minutes.
3 Cut the potatoes into wafer-thin slices. Add to the soup and simmer for another 5–10 minutes, or until the potato is tender. Season with salt and pepper. Serve sprinkled with parsley.

NUTRITION PER SERVE (6)
Protein 5 g; Fat 9 g; Carbohydrate 20 g; Dietary Fibre 4 g; Cholesterol 25 mg; 835 kJ (200 cal)

Cover the pan and sweat the onion rings over very low heat, until tender.

Add the sugar and stir occasionally over medium heat, until caramelized.

Use a sharp knife to cut the unpeeled potatoes into wafer-thin slices.

SAVOURY POTATO EMPANADAS

Preparation time: 1 hour 10 minutes
Total cooking time: 40 minutes
Serves 8

2 x 375 g (12 oz) frozen blocks
    puff pastry
extra virgin olive oil, for
    cooking
250 g (8 oz) onions, finely diced
4 spring onions, thinly sliced
3 cloves garlic, crushed
200 g (6½ oz) beef mince
2 teaspoons ground cumin
2 teaspoons dried oregano
250 g (8 oz) potatoes, peeled
    and cubed
2 eggs, hard-boiled
100 g (3½ oz) black olives,
    pitted and cut into quarters
1 egg, separated
pinch of paprika
pinch of sugar

1 Defrost the blocks of puff pastry while preparing the filling. In a heavy-based frying pan, heat 1 tablespoon of the extra virgin olive oil, add the onion and spring onion and cook, stirring, for 5 minutes. Stir in the crushed garlic and cook for another 3 minutes. Remove from the pan and set aside.
2 Heat another tablespoon of the oil in the pan, add the beef mince and stir over medium heat until browned, breaking up any lumps with a fork. Add the onion and stir well.
3 Add the cumin, oregano, and a teaspoon each of salt and pepper, and stir for another 2 minutes. Transfer to a bowl and allow to cool. Wipe out the pan with paper towels.

4 Heat 1 tablespoon of oil in the pan, add the potato and stir over high heat for 1 minute. Reduce the heat to low and stir for 5 minutes, or until tender. Transfer to a plate to cool. Gently mix the potato into the beef mixture. Finely chop the eggs and set aside. Preheat the oven to moderately hot 200°C (400°F/Gas 6).
5 Working with one block of pastry at a time, roll out each slab on a lightly floured surface until 2.5 mm (¹/8 inch) thick. Cut out rounds, using a 10 cm (4 inch) diameter cutter. Lightly grease 2 baking trays.
6 Spoon the beef mixture onto one side of the pastry rounds (leaving a clear border wide enough for the pastry to be folded over). Place a few olive slices and some chopped egg on top of the beef mixture. Brush the border of the pastry with the egg white. Carefully fold the pastry over to make a half moon shape, pressing firmly to seal. Press the edges with a floured fork, to decorate, and then gently transfer to the baking trays. Stir the egg yolk, paprika and sugar together and use to brush over the empanadas. Bake for 15 minutes, or until golden.

NUTRITION PER SERVE
Protein 15 g; Fat 30 g; Carbohydrate 50 g; Dietary Fibre 3 g; Cholesterol 115 mg; 2215 kJ (530 cal)

COOK'S FILE

Note: These popular Mexican and Spanish specialities are usually, but not always, single serving turnovers with a pastry crust and savoury filling. Traditionally, empanadas are eaten without sauces. Eat them straight from the oven, but be careful of the intense heat that steams out with the first bite.

Once the beef mince has browned, return the onion and garlic to the pan.

Mix together the beef and potato, and finely chop the hard-boiled egg.

Roll out the block of defrosted pastry on a lightly floured surface.

Spoon the filling onto the pastry rounds, leaving a wide border.

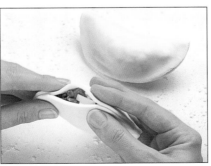
The egg white will help the pastry edges stick together when folded over.

Mix together the yolk, paprika and sugar and use to glaze the empanadas.

VICHYSSOISE

Preparation time: 25 minutes
Total cooking time: 30 minutes
Serves 4–6

60 g (2 oz) butter
2 leeks, chopped
2 large potatoes, peeled and
    chopped
3 cups (750 ml/24 fl oz) chicken
    stock

1 cup (250 ml/8 fl oz) milk
sour cream or cream, for serving
chopped chives, for serving

1 Melt the butter in a pan and cook the leek until soft. Add the potato and stock and simmer for 15–20 minutes, or until the potato is tender. Stir in the milk and season with salt and pepper.
2 Allow to cool a little before puréeing, in batches, in a blender or food processor, until smooth. Vichyssoise is traditionally served well-chilled, but if you prefer to serve it hot, return to the pan and reheat gently without boiling. Whether hot or chilled, spoon sour cream on top and sprinkle with chives to serve.

NUTRITION PER SERVE (6)
Protein 4 g; Fat 10 g; Carbohydrate 15 g; Dietary Fibre 2 g; Cholesterol 35 mg; 695 kJ (165 cal)

C O O K ' S   F I L E

Note: This is a classic soup, created by the Ritz-Carlton hotel in New York.

Cook the chopped leek in the melted butter until soft.

Add the milk to the potato mixture and stir through.

Process the cooled mixture in batches in a food processor or blender, until smooth.

THAI POTATO CAKES

Preparation time: 20 minutes
Total cooking time: 24 minutes
Serves 3–4

750 g (1 1/2 lb) waxy potatoes,
    peeled
1–2 small red chillies, finely
    chopped
8 cm (3 inch) piece lemon grass,
    white part only, finely chopped
1 cup (50 g/1 3/4 oz) chopped
    coriander leaves

8 spring onions, chopped
2 eggs, lightly beaten
3 tablespoons plain flour
oil, for cooking
sweet chilli sauce, for serving

1 Grate the potatoes, then put in the centre of a tea towel and squeeze to remove as much moisture as possible. Mix the potato in a bowl with the chilli, lemon grass, coriander leaves, spring onion, egg and flour.
2 Heat 1.5 cm (5/8 inch) of oil in a frying pan. Use 2 heaped tablespoons of mixture per cake and cook three or

four cakes at a time, for 3–4 minutes over medium heat. Turn and cook for another 3 minutes, or until crisp and cooked through. Drain on paper towels and keep warm while cooking the remaining mixture. Serve hot, with sweet chilli sauce.

NUTRITION PER SERVE (4)
Protein 9 g; Fat 15 g; Carbohydrate 30 g;
Dietary Fibre 4 g; Cholesterol 90 mg;
1340 kJ (320 cal)

COOK'S FILE

Note: Discard the tough outer leaves from the lemon grass.

Coarsely grate the potatoes before squeezing the moisture out.

Add the egg to the potato and other ingredients and mix through.

Turn the potato cakes over and cook until crisp and cooked through.

PAW PAW, CARROT AND GINGER SALAD WITH POTATO WAFERS

Preparation time: 30 minutes
Total cooking time: 5–7 minutes
Serves 4

2 cups (300 g/10 oz) grated
    carrot
3 tablespoons shredded fresh
    ginger
2 tablespoons soft brown sugar
250 g (8 oz) green paw paw
1/4 cup (60 ml/2 fl oz) lime juice
1 tablespoon fish sauce
1 tablespoon peanut oil
1 fresh chilli, finely chopped
2 tablespoons shredded mint
1 long potato, weighing about
    150 g (5 oz), peeled
1 long orange sweet potato,
    weighing about
    150 g (5 oz), peeled
vegetable oil, for deep-frying

1 Mix the grated carrot, shredded ginger and brown sugar in a bowl and set aside, at room temperature, while preparing the paw paw.
2 Cut the paw paw in half and remove the seeds and membrane. Peel, slice into matchsticks and transfer to a bowl.
3 Combine the lime juice, fish sauce, peanut oil, chilli and mint with the carrot and ginger in a small pan and heat through gently, until just warm.
4 Slice the potato and orange sweet potato, lengthways or widthways, very thinly, into wafers. Heat the oil to 180°C/350°F (a cube of bread will brown in 15 seconds) and have a bowl lined with paper towels, ready for the wafers. Cook a small handful of

wafers at a time for 10 seconds, or until crisp and golden, then transfer to the bowl to drain.
5 Mix the carrot and ginger with the paw paw and place a portion in the centre of each plate. Top with the

wafers, then add a little more salad and more wafers. Serve immediately.

NUTRITION PER SERVE
Protein 3 g; Fat 20 g; Carbohydrate 25 g; Dietary Fibre 5 g; Cholesterol 0 mg; 1205 kJ (290 cal)

Combine the grated carrot, shredded ginger and brown sugar in a bowl.

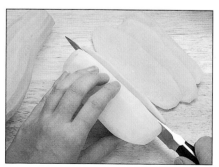

Cut the potato and sweet potato into wafter-thin slices.

Cook a few wafers at a time in the hot oil. They cook in about 10 seconds.

PEANUT AND POTATO CURRY

Preparation time: 30 minutes
Total cooking time: 1 hour 30 minutes
Serves 4–6

3 tablespoons oil
3 cloves garlic, finely chopped
2 red chillies, finely chopped
2 teaspoons ground coriander
1 teaspoon ground cumin
1/2 teaspoon ground fenugreek
   seeds
pinch each of ground cinnamon
   and nutmeg

2 onions, chopped
1.5 kg (3 lb) potatoes, peeled
   and cut into chunks
3/4 cup (125 g/4 oz) dry roasted
   peanuts, chopped
500 g (1 lb) very ripe tomatoes,
   chopped
1 teaspoon soft brown sugar
2 teaspoons finely grated
   lime rind
2 tablespoons lime juice
coriander leaves and roughly
   chopped peanuts, to garnish

1 Heat the oil in a large, deep pan or wok and stir-fry the garlic, chilli and spices over low heat for 3 minutes, or until very fragrant. Add the onion and cook for another 3 minutes.

2 Add the potato to the pan, tossing to coat with the spice mixture. Add 1/2 cup (125 ml/4 fl oz) water, cover and cook over low heat for 10 minutes, stirring regularly.

3 Add the peanuts and tomato, uncover and simmer for 1 hour 10 minutes, stirring occasionally. Season with the sugar, rind, juice and salt and pepper. Garnish with coriander and peanuts. Serve with rice.

NUTRITION PER SERVE (6)
Protein 15 g; Fat 20 g; Carbohydrate 40 g;
Dietary Fibre 7 g; Cholesterol 0 mg;
1720 kJ (410 cal)

Stir the garlic, chilli and spices in the hot oil until very fragrant.

Use two wooden spoons to toss the potato and thoroughly coat with the spices.

Add the chopped peanuts and tomato to the pan.

SEAFOOD CROQUETTES

Preparation time: about 1 hour
+ 2 hours refrigeration
Total cooking time: 40–50 minutes
Serves 8–10

1 kg (2 lb) floury potatoes,
   peeled and quartered
30 g (1 oz) butter
400 g (13 oz) perch fillets (or
   any white-fleshed boneless
   fish fillets)
300 g (10 oz) scallops
500 g (1 lb) raw prawns, peeled
   and deveined
2 tablespoons peanut oil
1¹/2 teaspoons fish sauce
¹/2 cup (125 ml/4 fl oz) Thai
   sweet chilli sauce
280 ml (9 fl oz) coconut cream
2 cups (60 g/2 oz) coriander
   leaves, finely chopped
3 tablespoons lime juice
2 stalks lemon grass, white
   parts only, chopped
1 tablespoon chopped chives
1 cup (125 g/4 oz) plain flour
4 eggs
¹/2 cup (45 g/1¹/2 oz) desiccated
   coconut, lightly toasted
2¹/2 cups (250 g/8 oz) dry
   breadcrumbs
vegetable oil, for deep-frying

1 Steam or boil the potato until tender. When cooked, drain and mash with the butter until smooth, then allow to cool.

2 Meanwhile, slice the fish into 2 cm (³/4 inch) wide pieces and clean the scallops, removing the small brown vein. Pat all the seafood dry with paper towels. Heat the peanut oil in a large heavy-based pan. Reduce the heat to medium, add the fish, scallops and prawns, in small batches, and cook for 2–3 minutes. Scallops and prawns take about 1 minute each side.

3 Return all the seafood to the pan, stir in the fish sauce and chilli sauce and reduce the heat to low. Add the coconut cream, coriander leaves, lime juice and lemon grass and leave to simmer gently for 10 minutes. Remove from the heat and allow to cool slightly. Strain through a sieve and reserve all the sauce.

4 Chop the seafood in a food processor in short bursts, being very careful not to purée it. Mix the seafood with the potato mash, chives and 2 tablespoons of the sauce.

5 Line 2 trays with greaseproof paper. To crumb the croquettes, place the flour on a tray, plate or sheet of greaseproof paper. Lightly beat the eggs in a bowl. Mix the coconut and breadcrumbs and put on a tray or plate. Roll 2 tablespoons of the seafood and potato mixture into a croquette shape. Roll lightly in the flour, dip in the egg and roll into the breadcrumb mix. Put on the lined trays. Cover with plastic wrap and refrigerate for 2 hours.

6 Warm the sauce and put into warm ramekins. Heat the oil to 180°C/350°F (a cube of bread dropped into the oil will brown in 15 seconds) in a deep-fryer or deep, heavy-based pan and deep-fry the croquettes, in batches, for 1–2 minutes, until golden. Make sure the oil doesn't get too hot and start smoking. Remove with a slotted spoon and drain on paper towels. Keep warm. Serve with the warmed sauce.

NUTRITION PER SERVE (10)
Protein 30 g; Fat 25 g; Carbohydrate 40 g; Dietary Fibre 4 g; Cholesterol 165 mg; 2125 kJ (510 cal)

Cook the fish pieces, scallops and prawns, in small batches, for 2–3 minutes.

Pour in the chilli sauce and fish sauce and stir over low heat.

Chop the seafood in a food processor, doing it in short bursts.

Shape 2 tablespoons of mixture into a croquette and roll in flour.

After dipping the croquettes in egg, roll them in the breadcrumb mix.

Remove the cooked croquettes from the oil with a slotted spoon.

LATKES

Preparation time: 35 minutes
Total cooking time: 30 minutes
Serves 4

1.5 kg (3 lb) waxy potatoes
1 tablespoon oil
1 egg, beaten
2 tablespoons plain flour
vegetable oil, for frying

1 Wash, peel and coarsely grate the potatoes. Rinse, drain thoroughly and wrap in a tea towel. Squeeze out the excess moisture and transfer the potato to a bowl.
2 Mix the grated potato with the oil and beaten egg. Season with salt and pepper and gently stir in the plain flour.
3 Make round flat cakes, using 2 tablespoons of mixture for each and shaping with floured hands. Shallow-

fry the pancakes in a large pan until golden brown on both sides. Drain on paper towels.

NUTRITION PER SERVE
Protein 10 g; Fat 20 g; Carbohydrate 55 g; Dietary Fibre 6 g; Cholesterol 45 mg; 1880 kJ (450 cal)

COOK'S FILE

Note: These potato pancakes are traditionally served hot, as a side dish, at Hanukkah, the Jewish festival.

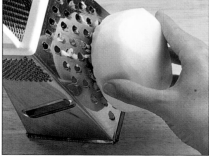

Grate the potatoes on the coarse side of the grater.

Mix the potato with the oil, beaten egg and flour.

Fry the potato cakes until golden brown on both sides.

BOULANGERE POTATOES

Preparation time: 35 minutes
Total cooking time: 1 hour
Serves 4–6

1 kg (2 lb) potatoes, peeled and
   very thinly sliced
2 cloves garlic, crushed
400 ml (13 fl oz) chicken or
   vegetable stock

1 Preheat the oven to moderately hot 200°C (400°F/Gas 6).
2 Thoroughly grease a 1-litre gratin dish and arrange a layer of overlapping potato slices in the base of the dish. Add a little of the crushed garlic and season with salt and pepper. Repeat the layers with the remaining potatoes.
3 Pour the stock of your choice over the potato and bake for 1 hour, uncovered, or until the potato is tender and the top crisp and brown.

NUTRITION PER SERVE (6)
Protein 4 g; Fat 1 g; Carbohydrate 20 g;
Dietary Fibre 3 g; Cholesterol 0 mg;
465 kJ (110 cal)

COOK'S FILE

Note: This is a French name meaning baker's potatoes. Last century, when many didn't have an oven, women prepared it and left it to be cooked at the local bakery during the day.

Peel the potatoes and slice very thinly with a sharp knife.

Grease a gratin dish and arrange a layer of potato in the base.

Pour the stock over the layered potato and garlic and bake for 1 hour.

POTATO AND CORIANDER SAMOSAS

Preparation time: 1 hour
Total cooking time: 30 minutes
Makes about 24

50 g (1³/₄ oz) butter
2 teaspoons grated fresh ginger
2 teaspoons cumin seeds
1 teaspoon Madras curry powder
¹/₂ teaspoon garam masala
500 g (1 lb) waxy potatoes,
    peeled and finely diced
¹/₄ cup (30 g/1 oz) sultanas
¹/₂ cup (80 g/2³/₄ oz) frozen
    baby peas
¹/₂ cup (15 g/¹/₂ oz) coriander
    leaves
3 spring onions, sliced
1 egg, lightly beaten
oil, for deep-frying
thick natural yoghurt, to serve

Samosa pastry
3³/₄ cups (465 g/15 oz) plain
    flour, sifted
1 teaspoon baking powder
1¹/₂ teaspoons salt
110 g (3¹/₂ oz) butter, melted
¹/₂ cup (125 g/4 oz) thick
    natural yoghurt

1 Heat the butter in a large non-stick frying pan, add the ginger, cumin seeds, curry powder and garam masala and fry lightly for 1 minute. Add the potato and 3 tablespoons water and cook over low heat for 15–20 minutes, or until the potato is tender. Toss the sultanas, peas, coriander leaves and spring onion through the potato, remove from the heat and set aside to cool.
2 To make the samosa pastry, combine the flour, baking powder and salt in a large bowl. Make a well in the centre, add the butter, yoghurt and ³/₄ cup (185 ml/6 fl oz) of water. Using a flat-bladed knife, bring the dough together. Turn out onto a lightly floured surface and bring together to form a smooth ball. Divide the dough into four to make it easier to work with. Roll one piece out until it is very thin. Cover the remaining pastry until you are ready to use it.
3 Using a 12 cm (5 inch) diameter bowl or plate as a guide, cut out six circles. Place a generous tablespoon of potato filling in the centre of each circle, brush the edges of the pastry with egg and fold over to form a semi-circle. Make repeated folds on the rounded edge by folding a little piece of the pastry back as you move around the edge. Continue with the remaining pastry and filling.
4 Heat the oil in a deep, heavy-based pan or deep-fryer, to 180°C/350°F (a cube of bread dropped into the oil will brown in 15 seconds). It is important not to have the oil too hot or the samosas will burn before the pastry has cooked. Add the samosas two or three at a time and cook until golden. If they rise to the surface as they puff up, you may need to use a large, long-handled slotted spoon to hold them in the oil to cook the other side. Drain on paper towels. Serve with yoghurt.

NUTRITION PER SAMOSA
Protein 3 g; Fat 6 g; Carbohydrate 20 g; Dietary Fibre 1 g; Cholesterol 15 mg; 570 kJ (135 cal)

COOK'S FILE

Hint: The samosa pastry becomes very tough if overworked. Use lightly floured hands when working the dough to prevent it sticking.

Toss the sultanas, peas, coriander leaves and spring onion through the potato.

Mix the butter, yoghurt and water into the flour mixture.

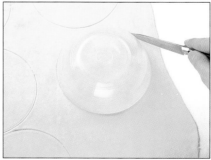

Cut six circles from each sheet of pastry, using a bowl or plate as a guide.

Use a generous tablespoon of mixture for each samosa.

Make folds on the edge of the pastry, folding a piece back as you move around.

Remove the cooked samosas from the oil with a slotted spoon.

CLAM CHOWDER

Preparation time: 35 minutes
Total cooking time: 45 minutes
Serves 4

1.5 kg (3 lb) fresh clams in shell
3 rashers bacon, chopped
1 onion, chopped
1 clove garlic, crushed
4 potatoes (about 750 g/1¹/2 lb),
**   peeled and cubed**
1¹/4 cups (315 ml/10 fl oz) fish
**   stock**
2 cups (500 ml/16 fl oz) milk
¹/2 cup (125 ml/4 fl oz) cream
3 tablespoons chopped parsley

1 Discard any clams that are already open (these should not be used). Put the rest in a large heavy-based pan with 1 cup (250 ml/8 fl oz) of water and simmer, covered, over low heat for 5 minutes, or until the shells open (discard any that do not open during cooking). Strain the liquid and reserve. Remove the clam meat from the shells.
2 Heat a little oil in the clean pan, add the bacon, onion and garlic and cook, stirring, until the onion is soft and the bacon golden. Add the potato and stir to combine.
3 Measure the reserved liquid and add enough water to make it up to 1¹/4 cups (315 ml/10 fl oz). Add to the pan with the stock and milk. Bring to

the boil, reduce the heat, cover and simmer for 20 minutes, or until the potato is tender. Uncover and simmer for 10 minutes, or until reduced and slightly thickened.
4 Add the cream, clam meat and parsley and season, to taste. Heat through gently before serving, but do not allow to boil or it may curdle.

NUTRITION PER SERVE
Protein 70 g; Fat 30 g; Carbohydrate 35 g; Dietary Fibre 4 g; Cholesterol 785 mg; 2850 kJ (680 cal)

COOK'S FILE

Variation: You can use canned clams, but drain before using and make up the liquid with fish stock.

Cook the clams for 5 minutes, then discard any which haven't opened.

Reserve the cooking liquid from the clams and remove the meat from the shells.

Add the cream, clam meat and parsley and season with salt and pepper, to taste.

POTATO PANCAKES WITH CREME FRAICHE

Preparation time: 20 minutes
Total cooking time: 20 minutes
Makes about 12

450 g (14 oz) floury potatoes, peeled and chopped
6 slices prosciutto
2 cups (250 g/8 oz) self-raising flour, sifted
1 teaspoon baking powder
1/2 cup (15 g/1/2 oz) chives, cut into long lengths
1/4 cup (10 g/1/3 oz) chopped parsley
1/2 cup (50 g/1³/4 oz) freshly grated Parmesan
80 g (2³/4 oz) butter, melted
2¹/2 cups (600 ml/20 fl oz) milk
crème fraîche or sour cream, for serving

1 Boil the potato until tender, drain and mash until smooth. Put the prosciutto on a baking tray, grill until crisp and allow to cool. Set aside.

2 Sift the flour and baking powder into a bowl. Add the chives, parsley, Parmesan and 1 teaspoon salt. Make a well in the centre, add the potato, butter and 2 cups (500 ml/16 fl oz) of milk and stir until combined. The mixture will thicken on standing, so if it is too thick to pour, add the remaining milk.

3 Wrap 30 g (1 oz) of butter in a piece of paper towel. Heat a non-stick frying pan and use the wrapped butter to lightly grease the pan. Pour 1/3 cup (80 g/2³/4 oz) of the mixture into the pan and cook over medium heat until bubbles appear on the surface and the underside is golden. Turn over and cook the other side. Continue with the remaining mixture, greasing between each pancake. Serve with prosciutto and crème fraîche or sour cream.

NUTRITION PER PANCAKE
Protein 8 g; Fat 10 g; Carbohydrate 20 g;
Dietary Fibre 2 g; Cholesterol 35 mg;
895 kJ (215 cal)

Put the prosciutto on a baking tray and grill until crisp.

Make a well in the centre and add the mashed potato, butter and milk.

Make pancakes, using 1/3 cup of the batter at a time.

FAMILY FAVOURITES

POTATO PIZZA

Preparation time: 40 minutes
Total cooking time: about 55 minutes
Serves 4

1 kg (2 lb) large brushed potatoes, peeled
2 cloves garlic, crushed
1/4 cup (60 g/2 oz) tomato paste
2 tablespoons bottled tomato pasta sauce
1 small chilli, finely chopped
2 tablespoons finely chopped parsley
150 g (5 oz) Cheddar cheese, grated
4 slices salami, cut in thin strips
3 Roma tomatoes, roughly chopped
120 g (4 oz) mushrooms, sliced
1 small red capsicum, thinly sliced
1 small onion, thinly sliced
oregano leaves

1 Preheat the oven to moderately hot 200°C (400°F/Gas 6). Lightly brush a 30 cm (12 inch) pizza tray with melted butter or oil. Cut the potatoes into thin slices and lay the slices, overlapping, on the prepared tray. Ensure the potato slices completely cover the tray and that there are no gaps. Combine a little olive oil and 1 clove of the crushed garlic and brush over the potato slices. Bake for 20 minutes. Remove, brush again with the remaining oil and garlic mixture and bake for another 15 minutes.

2 Combine the tomato paste, tomato pasta sauce, chilli, parsley, remaining crushed garlic and some salt and pepper in a bowl; mix well. Carefully spread this mixture over the cooked potato slices, avoiding moving any of the potato slices. Sprinkle a third of the grated cheese over the top.

3 Scatter half the salami, tomato, mushroom slices, capsicum and onion over the top, with another third of the cheese. Repeat this again with the remaining topping ingredients. Sprinkle the remaining cheese, some cracked pepper and the fresh oregano leaves over the top. Bake for 20 minutes or until the cheese has melted and the pizza is cooked through. Serve hot or warm.

NUTRITION PER SERVE
Protein 25 g; Fat 25 g; Carbohydrate 40 g; Dietary Fibre 8 g; Cholesterol 70 mg; 2045 kJ (490 cal)

Overlap the potato slices on the greased pizza tray.

Use a palette knife to spread the tomato mixture over the potato.

POTATO AND CARROT SOUP

Preparation time: 20 minutes
Total cooking time: 25–30 minutes
Serves 4

2 tablespoons oil
2 cloves garlic, crushed
1 onion, chopped
2 teaspoons ground cumin
1 teaspoon ground coriander
4 carrots, chopped
750 g (1¹/₂ lb) floury potatoes, peeled and chopped
4 cups (1 litre) vegetable stock
¹/₂ cup (125 ml/4 fl oz) cream
sour cream and coriander leaves, to garnish

1 Heat the oil in a heavy-based pan, add the garlic and onion and cook until softened. Add the cumin, coriander and ¹/₂ teaspoon of salt and cook for another minute. Add the carrot and potato and toss to coat. Add the stock to the pan and bring to the boil.

2 Reduce the heat and simmer for 20 minutes, or until the vegetables are tender. Cool slightly.

3 Process, in batches, until smooth, then return to the pan and heat gently. Stir in the cream. Serve garnished with sour cream and coriander leaves.

NUTRITION PER SERVE
Protein 5 g; Fat 25 g; Carbohydrate 40 g; Dietary Fibre 7 g; Cholesterol 40 mg; 1585 kJ (380 cal)

Cook the onion and garlic until softened, then add the cumin, coriander and salt.

Toss the carrot and potato in the onion and spice mixture, then add the stock.

Let the soup cool a little before processing to avoid any hot splashes.

POTATO AND POLENTA BREAD

Preparation time: 40 minutes
 + 1 hour 40 minutes standing
Total cooking time: 45 minutes
Makes 6 small loaves

**700 g (1 lb 7 oz) floury potatoes,
 peeled and chopped
2 teaspoons dried yeast
1¹/₄ cups (315 ml/10 fl oz) milk,
 warmed
100 g (3¹/₂ oz) butter, melted
1 egg, lightly beaten
2 teaspoons salt
up to 5 cups (625 g/1¹/₄ lb)
 plain flour, sifted
³/₄ cup (110 g/3¹/₂ oz) fine
 polenta plus 2 tablespoons,
 for sprinkling
milk, for glazing**

1 Boil or steam the potato until tender, then drain and mash until smooth. In a heatproof bowl, dissolve the yeast with the warmed milk. Leave in a warm place for 10 minutes.
2 Mix together the potato, yeast mixture, butter, egg, salt, 4 cups (500 g/1 lb) of the flour and the polenta. Bring together using your hands to form a soft dough.
3 Turn the dough out onto a lightly floured surface and knead for 10 minutes, or until it is smooth and elastic, adding extra flour if needed. Press with a finger to test: the dough will spring back and not leave an indent if it is ready. Place in a large lightly oiled bowl, cover and leave in a warm place for about 1 hour, or until doubled in size. Punch down the dough and knead for 5 minutes. Divide into six portions and shape each one into a smooth elongated ball. Put into six 2-cup (500 ml/16 fl oz) capacity oiled loaf tins and set aside in a warm place for 30 minutes.
4 Preheat the oven to moderate 180°C (350°F/Gas 4). Glaze the tops with milk and sprinkle with the extra polenta. Bake for 30–35 minutes, or until the tops are golden and the bread sounds hollow when tapped.

NUTRITION PER LOAF
Protein 20 g; Fat 20 g; Carbohydrate 125 g; Dietary Fibre 8 g; Cholesterol 80 mg; 3165 kJ (755 cal)

Place the yeast in a heatproof bowl and leave to dissolve in the warm milk.

Mix together the yeast mixture, potato, butter, egg, salt, flour and polenta.

Divide the dough into six portions, shape into smooth balls and place in the tins.

Glaze the tops of the loaves with milk and sprinkle with the extra polenta.

MIXED POTATO TARTS

Preparation time: 30 minutes
+ 30 minutes refrigeration
Total cooking time: 45 minutes
Serves 6

2 cups (250 g/8 oz) plain flour
1 teaspoon salt
125 g (4 oz) butter, cubed
1/2 cup (125 ml/4 fl oz) iced
    water

Filling
50 g (1³/4 oz) butter, melted
4 tablespoons oil
2 cloves garlic, crushed
1 tablespoon chopped parsley
4 medium leeks, thinly sliced
1/4 cup (60 g/2 oz) sour cream
2 tablespoons chopped herbs
250 g (8 oz) potatoes, unpeeled
250 g (8 oz) orange sweet
    potato, peeled
chopped chives, to garnish

1 Mix the flour, salt and butter in a food processor for 30 seconds, or until fine crumbs form. Add most of the water and process briefly until the mixture comes together. Add more water if the mixture is too dry. Turn out onto a lightly floured surface and bring together to form a smooth dough. Wrap with plastic wrap and refrigerate for 30 minutes.

2 To make the filling, mix the melted butter and 2 tablespoons of the oil with the garlic and parsley to make a garlic butter. Heat the remaining oil and 1 tablespoon of the garlic butter in a large frying pan, add the leek and cook over medium heat until the leek begins to turn golden. Set aside.

3 Preheat the oven to moderately hot 200°C (400°F/Gas 6). Divide the pastry into six and roll each piece out to fit a shallow 10 cm (4 inch) diameter lightly greased pie tin. Trim the edges and decorate with a fork. Prick the bases lightly and bake for 15 minutes, or until lightly golden. Allow to cool and then remove the pastry cases from the tins.

4 Mix together the sour cream and chopped fresh herbs and set aside. Thinly slice the potato and orange sweet potato. Heat a frying or chargrill pan and cook the slices, in

batches, until tender, lightly brushing with the garlic butter as you go.

5 Pile the leek into the pastry cases, then overlap the potato and sweet potato over the leek. Top with herbed cream and chives. Serve warm or cold.

NUTRITION PER SERVE
Protein 8 g; Fat 30 g; Carbohydrate 45 g; Dietary Fibre 5 g; Cholesterol 90 mg; 1950 kJ (465 cal)

Press the pastry into the tins, trim the edges and decorate with a fork.

Pile the leek into the pastry cases and top with the potato and sweet potato slices.

PEAR-SHAPED POTATO CROQUETTES

Preparation time: 1 hour
 + 1 hour 30 minutes refrigeration
Total cooking time: 20 minutes
Makes 12

600 g (1¼ lb) floury potatoes,
    peeled and chopped
1 egg
1 egg yolk
60 g (2 oz) Parmesan, grated
¼ cup (40 g/1¼ oz) finely
    chopped ham
¼ cup (15 g/½ oz) chopped
    parsley

1 small carrot
plain flour
1 egg, lightly beaten, extra
dry breadcrumbs
vegetable oil, for deep-frying

1 Cook the potato until tender, then drain and mash thoroughly. While the potato is still hot, gradually mash in the combined beaten egg and egg yolk, Parmesan, ham and parsley. Divide the mixture into 12 portions, put on a tray, cover with plastic wrap and refrigerate for at least 1 hour.
2 Cut the carrot into 12 long thin matchsticks and set aside. Shape the potato portions into small pear shapes and coat each in the flour, egg and

then the breadcrumbs. Put on a tray and refrigerate again for at least 30 minutes, to firm.
3 Heat the oil about 8 cm (3 inches) deep in a large pan. Fry the carrot sticks briefly until lightly browned, then drain on paper towels. Fry the potato pears, three or four at a time so the pan does not overcrowd, for 2 minutes, or until evenly browned. Drain on paper towels. With the aid of a skewer gently push a carrot stick into the top of each 'pear' to make the stalk. Serve hot or warm.

NUTRITION PER CROQUETTE
Protein 5 g; Fat 8 g; Carbohydrate 9 g; Dietary Fibre 1 g; Cholesterol 50 mg; 545 kJ (130 cal)

Cook the potato until tender, then drain and mash thoroughly.

Coat the potato croquettes in the flour, then the egg and then the breadcrumbs.

Once the croquettes are deep-fried, use a skewer to push in the carrot 'stalks'.

TWO-POTATO HERB FRITTATA

Preparation time: 25 minutes
Total cooking time: about 1 hour
Serve 4–6

2 small potatoes, unpeeled
   and diced
300 g (10 oz) orange sweet
   potato, peeled and diced
30 g (1 oz) butter
1 tablespoon olive oil

300 g (10 oz) sour cream
4 eggs
1 tablespoon each of chopped
   thyme, oregano and
   flat-leaf parsley
2 teaspoons chopped rosemary

1 Grease a 23 cm (9 inch) fluted flan dish. Boil or steam the potato and sweet potato until just tender. Drain, then allow to cool and dry out completely. Melt the butter and olive oil in a heavy-based pan. Add the vegetables and cook, turning often, until crisp and golden. Transfer to the flan dish. Preheat the oven to moderate 180°C (350°F/Gas 4).

2 Whisk together the sour cream and eggs until smooth. Whisk in the fresh herbs and season, to taste, with salt and freshly ground pepper. Pour the sour cream mixture over the top of the frittata and cook for 40 minutes, or until set.

NUTRITION PER SERVE (6)
Protein 6 g; Fat 30 g; Carbohydrate 10 g;
Dietary Fibre 1 g; Cholesterol 200 mg;
1405 kJ (335 cal)

Use a sharp knife to cut the potato and sweet potato into small dice.

Cook the potato and sweet potato, turning regularly, until crisp and golden.

Pour the sour cream mixture over the vegetables and cook until set.

Arrange the sliced potato in a square and sprinkle with spring onion.

Brush around the edge of the paper with the beaten egg white.

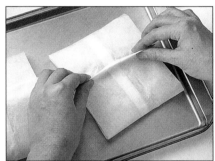

Fold the sides of the paper up and roll the edges over to form a parcel.

Place the parcels on a baking tray and bake for 30 minutes.

POTATOES IN PAPER PARCELS

Preparation time: 35 minutes
Total cooking time: 30 minutes
Serves 4

4 potatoes (about 200 g/
    6^1/$_2$ oz each), peeled
4 spring onions, thinly sliced
40 g (1^1/$_4$ oz) butter, chopped
small sprigs of rosemary
1 egg white, lightly beaten

1 Preheat the oven to moderate 180°C (350°F/Gas 4). Cut four 30 x 40 cm (12 x 16 inch) sheets of baking paper.

2 To assemble each parcel, thinly slice a potato and pat dry on a clean cloth. Arrange in two rows in a square in the centre of the paper. Sprinkle with a quarter of the spring onion, a quarter of the chopped butter, a few little sprigs of rosemary and some salt and freshly ground pepper.
3 Brush all around the outer edge of the baking paper with the egg white. Bring both the longer sides of the paper together and fold the ends over twice, using more egg white to seal. Fold the sides up into a parcel and seal with egg white. Repeat with the remaining parcels. Put on a baking tray and bake for 30 minutes. Carefully tear open the paper to serve.

NUTRITION PER SERVE
Protein 5 g; Fat 8 g; Carbohydrate 20 g;
Dietary Fibre 3 g; Cholesterol 25 mg;
745 kJ (180 cal)

POTATO AND CORN PARCELS

Preparation time: 1 hour
Total cooking time: 50 minutes
Makes 12

1.2 kg (2 lb 6½ oz) floury
   potatoes, peeled and chopped
250 g (8 oz) butter
2 leeks, thinly sliced
6 bacon rashers, rind removed,
   cut into thin strips
1 tablespoon finely chopped
   chives
200 g (6½ oz) frozen corn
   kernels
24 sheets fresh filo pastry
12 chives

1 Boil the potato until tender, then drain and mash with 30 g (1 oz) of the butter until smooth.

2 In a heavy-based pan, melt another 30 g (1 oz) of butter, add the leek and cook over medium heat for 5 minutes, or until soft and lightly golden. Remove from the pan and set aside. Add the bacon to the pan, increase the heat and stir for 5 minutes, or until browned. Mix into the potato with the leek and chopped chives.

3 Cook the corn in boiling water for 1–2 minutes, drain and add to the potato. Season with salt and pepper.

4 Melt the remaining butter and use to very lightly grease a 12-hole muffin tray (or two 6-hole trays) with medium-sized holes. Remove two sheets of filo pastry and cover the rest with a damp tea towel to prevent them drying out. Cut the two sheets in half, lightly brush each half with butter and carefully layer them on top of one another, making a pile of four half sheets for each parcel. Preheat the oven to moderate 180°C (350°F/Gas 4).

5 Put about ⅓ cup (100 g/3½ oz) of the potato filling into the centre of each pile of filo pastry and lift the corners to form a pouch. Tie a chive around each parcel and scrunch up the top gently. Bake in the muffin tin, in batches if necessary, for 15–20 minutes, or until golden.

NUTRITION PER PARCEL
Protein 8 g; Fat 20 g; Carbohydrate 20 g; Dietary Fibre 2 g; Cholesterol 60 mg; 1195 kJ (285 cal)

Mix together the mashed potato, leek, bacon, chives and corn.

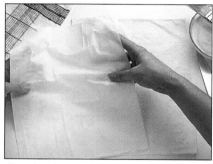

Cut the sheets of filo in half, brush with butter, and layer on top of each other.

Measure about a third of a cup of potato filling into the centre of the pastry.

Tie a chive around each parcel and bake them in the muffin tin.

HASH HAM CAKE

Preparation time: 30 minutes
  + 1 hour refrigeration
Total cooking time: 50 minutes
Serves 4–6

**500 g (1 lb) floury potatoes,
  peeled and quartered**
**200 g (6¹/₂ oz) ham, finely
  chopped**
4 spring onions, finely chopped
1 small gherkin, finely chopped

2 tablespoons chopped parsley
1 egg, lightly beaten
50 g (1³/₄ oz) butter

1 Cook the potato until tender. Drain and mash in a large bowl.
2 Mix in the ham, spring onion, gherkin, parsley, beaten egg and a generous amount of freshly ground black pepper. Spread on a plate, cover and refrigerate for at least 1 hour, or overnight, to firm.
3 Heat 30 g (1 oz) of the butter in a 23 cm (9 inch) heavy-based frying pan.

Add the potato mixture, spread evenly into the pan and smooth the surface with the back of a spoon. Cook over moderate heat for 15 minutes, then slide out onto a plate. Add the remaining butter to the pan, carefully flip the cake back into the pan and cook for another 15–20 minutes, or until the outside forms a brown crust. Serve hot, cut into wedges.

NUTRITION PER SERVE (6)
Protein 9 g; Fat 10 g; Carbohydrate 10 g; Dietary Fibre 2 g; Cholesterol 70 mg; 730 kJ (175 cal)

Spread the mixture on a plate, cover and refrigerate for at least 1 hour.

Spread the mixture in a heavy-based frying pan and smooth the surface.

Slide the hash cake onto a plate, then flip back into the pan to cook the other side.

POTATO CRUMBLE

Preparation time: 35 minutes
Total cooking time: 50 minutes
Serves 4–6

1 kg (2 lb) floury potatoes,
    peeled and quartered
100 g (3½ oz) butter
10 spring onions, finely sliced
2 cloves garlic, crushed
⅓ cup (80 ml/2¾ fl oz) milk

2 cups (160 g/5½ oz) fresh
    coarse breadcrumbs
3 tablespoons grated Cheddar
2 tablespoons chopped parsley

1 Preheat the oven to moderately hot 200°C (400°F/Gas 6). Boil the potato until tender, drain and return to the pan, then mash until smooth.
2 Melt half the butter in a small pan and add a tablespoon of oil. Cook the spring onion and garlic until soft, then add to the mashed potato with the milk. Mash together until smooth. Spoon into a shallow casserole dish and smooth the top.
3 To make the crumble, melt the remaining butter and mix with the breadcrumbs, cheese and parsley. Sprinkle over the potato mixture. Bake for 20 minutes, or until the crumble is golden and crispy.

NUTRITION PER SERVE (6)
Protein 10 g; Fat 20 g; Carbohydrate 40 g; Dietary Fibre 5 g; Cholesterol 50 mg; 1560 kJ (375 cal)

Add the spring onion and garlic to the mashed potato with the milk.

Spoon into a shallow casserole dish and smooth the surface.

Melt the remaining butter and mix with the breadcrumbs, cheese and parsley.

GREEN PEA, POTATO AND SHALLOT SOUP

Preparation time: 30 minutes
Total cooking time: 45 minutes
Serves 6

350 g (11 oz) shelled fresh peas
350 g (11 oz) potatoes, peeled
    and cubed
5 cups (1.25 litres) chicken stock
2 tablespoons olive oil
30 g (1 oz) butter
5 French shallots
pinch of nutmeg
3–4 tablespoons grated Parmesan

1 Put the peas and potato in a large pan and add about 750 ml (24 fl oz) of the stock. Bring to the boil, reduce the heat and simmer for 25 minutes, or until the vegetables are tender.
2 Slice 3 of the shallots thinly. Heat the oil and butter in a pan, add the sliced shallots and stir until softened. Remove and set aside to use as a garnish. Chop the remaining shallots, add to the pan and stir over medium heat until softened, but not browned. Pour in the remaining chicken stock.
3 Purée the peas and potato with any stock left in the pan, then return to the pan and pour in the fried shallots and stock. Bring to the boil, add the nutmeg and season. Reduce the heat and simmer for 5 minutes, stirring occasionally, until blended. Stir in the Parmesan and garnish with the shallots.

NUTRITION PER SERVE
Protein 7 g; Fat 15 g; Carbohydrate 10 g; Dietary Fibre 5 g; Cholesterol 20 mg; 800 kJ (190 cal)

COOK'S FILE

Note: French shallots look like very small brown onions. You can use Asian shallots, which look more like red-skinned garlic cloves and are much smaller than the French type. Use 3 tablespoons sliced (to garnish) and 2 tablespoons chopped.

Put the peas and potato in a large pan and cook in the stock.

Heat the oil and butter in a pan and cook the sliced shallots until softened.

Return the puréed soup to the pan and stir in the fried shallots and stock.

***Potato crumble (top)
with Green pea, potato and shallot soup***

NEW POTATO, CHICKEN AND SPINACH FRITTATA

Preparation time: 30 minutes
Total cooking time: 1 hour 5 minutes
Serves 4–6

600 g (1¼ lb) new potatoes,
   unpeeled, sliced
   about 1 cm (½ inch) thick
1 small barbecued chicken
500 g (1 lb) English spinach
   leaves, stalks removed
125 g (4 oz) feta, crumbled
½ cup (50 g/1¾ oz) grated
   Parmesan
½ cup (15 g/½ oz) basil leaves,
   chopped
10 eggs, lightly beaten
12 semi-dried tomato quarters

1 Preheat the oven to moderate 180°C (350 F/Gas 4). Put the potato in a greased ovenproof dish, brush all over with a little oil and bake for 30 minutes, or until cooked. Turn the potato once or twice during baking. Allow to cool.

2 Remove the skin from the chicken, pull the flesh from the bones and roughly chop the meat.

3 Wash the spinach, put in a large pan, cover and steam for 2 minutes to wilt slightly. Drain and allow to cool, then squeeze out the moisture and chop. Mix with the chicken and stir in the feta, Parmesan and basil. Season with salt and pepper, to taste.

4 Brush a 24 cm (9½ inch) diameter non-stick pan with a little oil. Arrange half the potato slices over the base and spread half the chicken mixture on top, then repeat the layers. Season the beaten egg and pour over the top.

Arrange the tomato quarters on top. Cook over low heat for 25 minutes, or until the centre is almost cooked. Take care not to burn the base. Heat the frittata under a grill for 7 minutes, or until set. Cut into wedges to serve.

NUTRITION PER SERVE (6)
Protein 40 g; Fat 25 g; Carbohydrate15 g; Dietary Fibre 4 g; Cholesterol 375 mg; 2080 kJ (500 cal)

Steam the spinach leaves for 2 minutes, then squeeze out all the moisture.

Build up the layers of sliced potato and chicken filling.

Place the frittata under a preheated grill until it has set.

VINEGAR POTATOES

Preparation time: 30 minutes
Total cooking time: 2 hours
Serves 4

8 small white onions
2 parsnips
12 small round chat potatoes
6 sprigs of rosemary
3 tablespoons balsamic vinegar
90 g (3 oz) butter, melted

1 Preheat the oven to moderate 180°C (350°F/Gas 4). Peel the onions and cut into quarters, leaving a small amount of stalk to keep the onion together. Peel the parsnips and cut into short, thick sticks.

2 Put the vegetables and rosemary in a baking dish that is just large enough to hold all the vegetables in a single layer. Pour the balsamic vinegar and butter over them and toss until well coated. Season with 1/2 teaspoon each of salt and freshly ground black pepper. Bake for 2 hours, stirring the vegetables every 30 minutes to re-coat in butter and vinegar.

3 When ready to serve, remove the rosemary and replace with fresh sprigs, for garnishing.

NUTRITION PER SERVE
Protein 8 g; Fat 20 g; Carbohydrate 40 g; Dietary Fibre 7 g; Cholesterol 60 mg; 1465 kJ (350 cal)

COOK'S FILE

Hint: Use pearl onions if available.

Peel the onions and cut into quarters, leaving the stalk to keep them together.

Peel the parsnips and cut into short thick sticks for roasting.

Stir the vegetables every 30 minutes, basting with the butter and vinegar.

POTATO AND SALAMI BAKE

Preparation time: 35 minutes
Total cooking time: 1 hour 30 minutes
Serves 4–6

³/4 cup (60 g/2 oz) fresh
   breadcrumbs
1.25 kg (2¹/2 lb) floury potatoes,
   peeled and thinly sliced
125 g (4 oz) sliced salami
¹/2 cup (125 ml/4 fl oz) cream
3 eggs, lightly beaten
2 tablespoons plain flour
1 tablespoon chopped parsley
2 tablespoons chopped chives
3 tablespoons grated Parmesan
30 g (1 oz) cold butter, cubed

1 Preheat the oven to moderate 180°C (350°F/Gas 4). Grease a 20 cm (8 inch) round springform tin and use about a third of the breadcrumbs to coat the base and side.

2 Layer half the potato, overlapping slightly, in the tin. Arrange the salami in a layer, then finish with the remaining potato.

3 Beat together the cream, eggs, flour, parsley, chives and some salt and pepper. Pour over the potato, cover with foil and bake for 1 hour 20 minutes. Remove the foil and scatter with the combined remaining breadcrumbs, Parmesan and butter. Bake for 10–15 minutes, until tender.

NUTRITION PER SERVE (6)
Protein 15 g; Fat 25 g; Carbohydrate 40 g; Dietary Fibre 4 g; Cholesterol 160 mg; 1880 kJ (450 cal)

Coat the base and side of the greased tin with breadcrumbs.

Layer half the potato in the base of the prepared tin.

Remove the foil and scatter with the breadcrumbs, Parmesan and butter.

POTATO PARCELS WITH BACON AND MUSHROOMS

Preparation time: 1 hour
+ 20 minutes resting
Total cooking time: 50–60 minutes
Serves 4

450 g (14 oz) floury potatoes,
    peeled and chopped
1 teaspoon salt
70 g (2$\frac{1}{4}$ oz) butter, softened
200 g (6$\frac{1}{2}$ oz) plain flour
100 g (3$\frac{1}{2}$ oz) bacon rashers,
    rind removed, cut into
    thin strips
1 small onion, finely chopped
1 clove garlic, crushed
100 g (3$\frac{1}{2}$ oz) button
    mushrooms, thinly sliced
pinch of cayenne
1 tablespoon sour cream
1 tablespoon chopped flat-leaf
    parsley
vegetable oil, for frying

1 To make the pastry, cook the potato until tender. Drain and set aside for 20 minutes. Mash until smooth. Do not process. Stir in the salt and 50 g (1$\frac{3}{4}$ oz) of the butter, then work in enough flour to give a soft but dry dough. Knead twelve to fifteen times before setting aside, covered with a dry tea towel.

2 To make the filling, heat a little oil in a pan, add the bacon, onion and garlic and stir over medium heat for 2 minutes, or until the onion is soft. Add the remaining butter and the mushrooms and cook for 5 minutes. Add the cayenne and some black pepper. Stir in the sour cream and parsley. Remove from the heat.

3 Divide the dough into four portions (it is quite delicate to work with). Roll each out into a sheet, about 3 mm (1/8 inch) thick, on a well-floured work surface. Using an 8 cm (3 inch) round biscuit cutter, cut out six circles from each dough portion. Gather together the leftover dough and repeat this. Allow the dough to rest a little as it becomes quite elastic. Brush around the edge of half the circles with water, then divide the filling among them.

Cover each with another circle of dough and press the edges together firmly to seal.

4 Heat 3–4 tablespoons of oil in a frying pan and cook the parcels, in batches, over medium heat for 5 minutes, or until golden on each side. Add more oil as needed. Serve warm.

NUTRITION PER SERVE
Protein 15 g; Fat 30 g; Carbohydrate 55 g; Dietary Fibre 5 g; Cholesterol 60 mg; 2330 kJ (555 cal)

Divide the dough into four portions, then cut six rounds from each portion.

Brush the edge of each round with water and then spoon on the filling.

Cook the parcels in batches so that the pan does not overcrowd.

67

ZUCCHINI, POTATO AND OREGANO PANCAKES

Preparation time: 30 minutes
Total cooking time: 30 minutes
Serves 4

500 g (1 lb) waxy potatoes, peeled
500 g (1 lb) zucchini
2 cloves garlic, finely chopped
2 onions, finely chopped
2 cups (250 g/8 oz) self-raising
　　flour
2 eggs, lightly beaten
1/2 cup (125 ml/4 fl oz) milk
30 g (1 oz) melted butter
2 tablespoons each of chopped
　　parsley, sage and oregano
100 g (3½ oz) sour cream

Tomato sauce
500 ml (16 fl oz) good-quality
　　bottled tomato pasta sauce
2 teaspoons soft brown sugar
2 teaspoons chopped fresh chilli
1 tablespoon balsamic vinegar

1 Grate the potato and zucchini. Mix in a bowl with the garlic, onion, flour, eggs, milk, melted butter, fresh herbs and 1 teaspoon each of salt and pepper.

2 Preheat the oven to slow 150°C (300°F/Gas 2) and brush a large heavy-based pan with oil. Heat the pan over medium heat and, using 1/3 cup (80 ml/2¾ fl oz) of batter for each pancake, cook in batches over medium-low heat, for 2–3 minutes each side, until the pancakes are golden brown and quite puffy. Transfer to a heatproof dish and keep warm in a low oven while cooking the remainder.

3 To make the tomato sauce, combine all the ingredients in a pan with salt and pepper, to taste. Bring the mixture to the boil, then reduce the heat and simmer for 10 minutes, stirring occasionally to prevent it catching on the base of the pan.

4 Serve drizzled with tomato sauce and with a spoonful of sour cream.

NUTRITION PER SERVE
Protein 20 g; Fat 20 g; Carbohydrate 85 g; Dietary Fibre 10 g; Cholesterol 150 mg; 2580 kJ (615 cal)

Grate the potato and zucchini and put them into a large bowl.

Use about one third of a cup of batter to make each pancake.

Put all the tomato sauce ingredients in a pan and season, to taste.

SALMON PATTIES

Preparation time: 1 hour
Total cooking time: 25 minutes
Serves 4

650 g (1 lb 5 oz) floury
    potatoes, peeled
425 g (14 oz) can red salmon,
    drained, bones and
    skin removed
2 spring onions, finely chopped
1/4 cup (15 g/1/2 oz) chopped
    fresh parsley
2 teaspoons grated lemon rind

1 egg
5 slices multi-grain bread,
    crusts removed
40 g (1 1/4 oz) butter
3 tablespoons olive oil

1 Cut the potatoes into chunks and cook until very tender. Drain well and mash until smooth.
2 Place the salmon in a large bowl and break up the flesh with a fork. Add the spring onion, parsley, lemon rind, egg and mashed potato. Add salt and pepper, to taste, and stir well. Shape into rough patties, using about one third of a cup for each patty.

3 Chop the bread in a food processor until fine crumbs are formed. Gently roll the patties in the breadcrumbs and neaten the shape. Press the breadcrumbs firmly onto the patties, so they coat well.
4 Place the butter and oil in a large frying pan. When the butter is foaming, add the patties and cook each side for 3–5 minutes or until golden and browned. Drain on paper towels. Serve with lemon wedges.

NUTRITION PER SERVE
Protein 35 g; Fat 40 g; Carbohydrate 40 g; Dietary Fibre 5 g; Cholesterol 150 mg; 2640 kJ (630 cal)

Mix the salmon with the spring onion, parsley, rind, egg and potato.

To make fresh breadcrumbs, simply chop slices of bread in a food processor.

Firmly press the breadcrumbs onto the salmon patties.

LEEK AND POTATO RAGU

Preparation time: 25 minutes
Total cooking time: 45 minutes
Serves 4–6

50 g (1³⁄4 oz) butter
2 tablespoons olive oil
**250 g (8 oz) piece double-
  smoked ham, cut into cubes**
3 cloves garlic, finely chopped
3 medium leeks, sliced
**1.5 kg (3 lb) potatoes, peeled
  and cut into large chunks**

500 ml (16 fl oz) chicken stock
2 tablespoons brandy
¹⁄2 cup (125 ml/4 fl oz) cream
**1 tablespoon each of chopped
  oregano and parsley**

1 Heat the butter and oil in a large heavy-based pan. Cook the ham, garlic and leek over low heat for 10 minutes, stirring regularly.
2 Add the potato and cook for 10 minutes, stirring regularly.
3 Slowly stir in the combined stock and brandy. Cover and bring to a gentle simmer. Cook for another 15–20 minutes, or until the potato is very tender but still chunky, and the sauce has thickened. Add the cream and herbs and season with salt and pepper. Simmer for another 5 minutes. Serve with toast.

NUTRITION PER SERVE (6)
Protein 15 g; Fat 25 g; Carbohydrate 40 g; Dietary Fibre 9 g; Cholesterol 70 mg; 1990 kJ (475 cal)

C O O K ' S   F I L E

Note: You can use any type of ham for this recipe. A double smoked ham will give a good flavour.

Heat the butter and oil in a pan, then cook the ham, garlic and leek.

Stir in the stock and brandy, then cover and leave to simmer.

Once the sauce has thickened, add the cream and chopped herbs.

Cook the onion over low heat, very slowly so that it caramelizes.

Cut the capsicums into quarters and grill until blackened and blistered.

Deep-fry the chips in hot oil, until they are cooked but not browned.

Cook the tortilla until the underside is golden, then flip over.

EGG AND VEGETABLE TORTILLAS

Preparation time: 1 hour 30 minutes
Total cooking time: 1 hour
Serves 4–6

1 tablespoon extra virgin
  olive oil
2 red onions, finely sliced
1 clove garlic, crushed
90 g (3 oz) English spinach,
  roughly chopped
2 red capsicums
1 kg (2 lb) potatoes, cut into
  shoestring chips
vegetable oil, for deep-frying
6 eggs, beaten
3 tablespoons of combined
  chopped herbs (basil,
  parsley and oregano)

1 Heat the oil in a heavy–based pan and stir the onions over high heat for 2–3 minutes. Reduce the heat and cook for 30–40 minutes, until the onion starts to caramelize and break down. Increase the heat slightly, add the garlic and stir for 1 minute. Add the spinach, toss through and cook for another minute.

2 Cut the capsicums into quarters and remove the seeds and membrane. Grill, skin-side-up, until the skin is blackened and blistered. Cover with a damp tea towel until cooled. Peel and slice the flesh into fine strips.

3 Heat the oil to 160°C/315°F (a cube of bread will brown in 30 seconds) and deep-fry the chips until cooked but not brown. Remove and drain on paper towels. In a bowl, mix the onion, spinach, capsicum and chips.

4 Combine the eggs and herbs, add to the vegetables and toss through. Lightly grease a small 20 cm (8 inch) frying pan and add enough of the tortilla mixture to cover the base of the pan. Cook over medium heat for 2–3 minutes, until the underside is golden. Flip and cook the other side. Keep warm while cooking the remaining tortilla mixture.

NUTRITION PER SERVE (6)
Protein 15 g; Fat 20 g; Carbohydrate 25 g; Dietary Fibre 5 g; Cholesterol 180 mg; 1350 kJ (325 cal)

POTATO AND SALMON PARCELS

Preparation time: 30 minutes
Total cooking time: 40 minutes
Serves 4

750 g (1½ lb) floury potatoes,
   peeled
40 g (1¼ oz) butter
¼ cup (60 ml/2 fl oz) cream
1 cup (125 g/4 oz) grated
   Cheddar cheese
210 g (7 oz) can red salmon,
   skin and bones removed,
   flaked
1 tablespoon chopped dill
4 spring onions, finely
   chopped
3 sheets ready-rolled
   puff pastry
beaten egg, for glazing

1 Cut the potatoes into small pieces and cook in a pan of boiling water until tender. Mash with the butter and the cream until there are no lumps. Lightly grease two oven trays.

2 Add the cheese, salmon, dill and spring onion to the potato and mix well. Preheat the oven to moderately hot 200°C (400°F/Gas 6). Cut each pastry sheet into four squares. Divide the mixture among the squares (approximately ¼ cup in each). Lightly brush the edges with beaten egg. Bring all four corners to the centre to form a point and press together to make a parcel.

3 Put the parcels on the greased trays and glaze with egg. Bake for 15–20 minutes, or until the pastry is golden brown.

NUTRITION PER SERVE
Protein 30 g; Fat 55 g; Carbohydrate 70 g; Dietary Fibre 5 g; Cholesterol 180 mg; 3700 kJ (885 cal)

COOK'S FILE

Note: Before removing the pastries from the oven, lift them gently off the tray and check the bottom of the parcels to make sure the pastry is cooked through. Take care not to overcook the parcels or they may burst open.

If you would like your puff to taste extra buttery, brush it with melted butter before baking it.

Cook and drain the potato, then mash well with the butter and cream.

Mix the cheese, salmon, dill and spring onion into the mashed potato.

Cut each pastry sheet into four squares and then divide the filling among them.

Bring up the corners to the centre and press together to make a parcel.

ROAST POTATO WITH BABY BEETS

Preparation time: 25 minutes
Total cooking time: about 1 hour
Serves 4–6

1 kg (2 lb) potatoes, unpeeled, cut in chunks
6 tablespoons olive oil
200 g (6½ oz) baby beetroots
2 tablespoons wholegrain mustard
1 clove garlic, finely chopped
1–2 tablespoons lemon juice
1 teaspoons finely grated lemon rind
2 tablespoons chopped chives
50 g (1¾ oz) snow pea sprouts, ends trimmed

1 Preheat the oven to moderate 180°C (350°F/Gas 4). Put the potatoes in a baking dish, drizzle with half the oil and sprinkle with 1 teaspoon of salt. Bake for 30 minutes, shaking the pan and carefully turning the potato over occasionally.

2 Trim and discard the beetroot tops, leaving a small amount of stalk attached. Brush the beetroot and wash well. Add to the potato, toss and bake for another 20–30 minutes, or until the potato is crisp and the beets tender. Allow to cool.

3 Whisk together the remaining oil, mustard, garlic, lemon juice and rind, and some salt and pepper. To serve, put the potato and beets on a platter or in a large bowl, drizzle with the dressing and scatter with chives. Top with the sprouts. Serve warm.

NUTRITION PER SERVE (6)
Protein 5 g; Fat 20 g; Carbohydrate 25 g; Dietary Fibre 4 g; Cholesterol 0 mg; 1250 kJ (300 cal)

Trim the top of the beetroot but leave the stalk intact, or it will bleed.

Add the beetroot to the potato and bake for another 20–30 minutes.

Whisk together the dressing ingredients, then drizzle over the roast vegetables.

POTATO AND CELERIAC SOUP

Preparation time: 35 minutes
Total cooking time: 30 minutes
Serves 4–6

400 g (13 oz) celeriac
1 tablespoon lemon juice
2 tablespoons oil
40 g (1¼ oz) butter
1 large onion, finely
    chopped
1 clove garlic, finely chopped

750 g (1½ lb) floury potatoes,
    peeled and cubed
2 tablespoons plain flour
3 cups (750 ml/24 fl oz)
    vegetable stock or water
¼ cup (125 ml/4 fl oz) cream
pinch of ground cinnamon

1 Peel and cube the celeriac and put in a bowl of water with a tablespoon of lemon juice, to prevent browning. Heat the oil and butter in a large heavy-based pan and cook the onion and garlic for 5 minutes. Add the potato and drained celeriac, cover and cook for 8 minutes, stirring regularly.
2 Add the flour to the pan and stir. Cook for 2 minutes and add the stock. Season, bring to the boil, lower the heat and simmer, uncovered, for 10 minutes or until the vegetables are tender. Add the cream and cinnamon.
3 Purée in batches in a food processor, return to the pan, add 1 cup (250 ml/ 8 fl oz) water and heat thoroughly. Garnish with chives and pepper.

NUTRITION PER SERVE (6)
Protein 6 g; Fat 20 g; Carbohydrate 25 g; Dietary Fibre 6 g; Cholesterol 45 mg; 1300 kJ (310 cal)

Cook the onion and garlic, then add the potato and celeriac.

Add the flour to the vegetables in the pan and stir well.

Pour in the stock, season to taste and bring to the boil.

Peel the potatoes and cut into very fine slices with a sharp knife.

Coat the potato slices in the seasoned flour so they get a crisp finish.

Deep-fry the potato chips in batches so the pan isn't too crowded.

Mix together the ingredients to make the chilli cream.

SPICED POTATO CHIPS WITH CHILLI CREAM

Preparation time: 40 minutes
Total cooking time: 15–20 minutes
Serves 4

1/2 cup (60 g/2 oz) plain flour
2 teaspoons chicken salt
3 teaspoons ground cumin
1/2 teaspoon garam masala
1/2 teaspoon mustard powder
3 large potatoes, peeled
oil, for deep-frying
3–4 cloves garlic, peeled
2/3 cup (170 g/5 1/2 oz) sour cream
2 tablespoons chopped
    coriander
grated rind of 1 lime
2–3 teaspoons sweet chilli sauce

1 Mix the flour, chicken salt, cumin, garam masala, mustard powder and 1/2 teaspoon of black pepper in a large bowl. Cut the potatoes into wafer thin slices with a sharp knife.
2 Half fill a large pan with oil, add the garlic cloves and heat until the oil is moderately hot. Test the oil with a small cube of bread. If it sizzles immediately, it is ready. Remove the garlic if it gets too brown.
3 Toss the potato in the seasoned flour and cook in batches until crisp and golden. Drain on paper towels.
4 To make the chilli cream, combine the sour cream, coriander, rind and chilli sauce and serve with the chips.

NUTRITION PER SERVE
Protein 8 g; Fat 30 g; Carbohydrate 40 g; Dietary Fibre 5 g; Cholesterol 50 mg; 1920 kJ (460 cal)

COOK'S FILE

Note: The potatoes must be cut very thinly to become crisp. Use a mandolin if you have one.

POTATO AND SPICED SAUSAGE BAKE

Preparation time: 30 minutes
Total cooking time: 45 minutes
Serves 4

50 g (1³/4 oz) butter
2 tablespoons olive oil
1.5 kg (3 lb) potatoes, peeled
    and cubed
4 cloves garlic, roughly chopped
³/4 cup (185 ml/6 fl oz) cream
150 g (5 oz) Gruyère cheese

4 bratwurst sausages (about
    250 g/8 oz)
¹/2 teaspoon sweet paprika
2 tablespoons chopped parsley

1 Heat the butter and oil in a large heavy-based frying pan. Add the potato and garlic and toss over the heat for 10 minutes. Cover and cook for 10 minutes, again tossing regularly. The potato should be crisp on the outside and soft in the centre.

2 Drizzle the cream over the top, increase the heat to high and cook for 5 minutes, tossing until the cream is absorbed. Grate the cheese and add to the pan with salt and pepper, to taste. Spoon into a deep casserole dish, set aside and keep warm.

3 Preheat the oven to moderate 180°C (350°F/Gas 4). Prick the sausages and fry for 5–6 minutes, or until brown. Cut into slices, layer over the potato and sprinkle with paprika. Bake for 8 minutes. Sprinkle with the parsley to serve.

NUTRITION PER SERVE
Protein 35 g; Fat 75 g; Carbohydrate 50 g; Dietary Fibre 7 g; Cholesterol 180 mg; 4260 kJ (1015 cal)

Cook the potato until crisp, then pour on the cream and toss until absorbed.

Prick the sausages so they do not burst, then fry until brown.

Slice the bratwurst and arrange over the top of the potato.

Roll out the pastry and use to line the base and side of the tin.

Use a steamer to lightly cook the vegetables, or simmer until just tender.

Build up the layers of potato and onion, pressing them together.

Mix together the cream, egg and mustard and pour over the tart.

SWEET POTATO, POTATO AND ONION TART

Preparation time: 45 minutes
+ 15 minutes refrigeration
Total cooking time: 1 hour 10 minutes
Serves 4–6

1 cup (125 g/4 oz) plain flour
90 g (3 oz) butter, chopped
500 g (1 lb) orange sweet
    potato, peeled
500 g (1 lb) potatoes, peeled
1 large onion, thinly sliced
1 cup (250 ml/8 fl oz) cream
2 eggs
1 tablespoon wholegrain
    mustard

1 To make the pastry, mix the flour and butter in a food processor until mixture resembles fine breadcrumbs. Add 1–2 tablespoons of water and process for 5 seconds to combine. Turn out onto a lightly floured surface and gather into a smooth ball.

2 Roll out the pastry on a sheet of baking paper large enough to fit the base and sides of a 23 cm (9 inch) flan tin. Ease the pastry into the tin, trim the edge and chill for 15 minutes. Preheat the oven to moderately hot 190°C (375°F/Gas 5).

3 Cover the pastry with a piece of greaseproof paper, fill with dried rice or beans and bake for 10 minutes. Discard the paper and rice and bake for another 10 minutes. Cool slightly.

4 Thinly slice the sweet potato and potato. Cook in a steamer for 15 minutes, or until just tender. Drain off any liquid, cover and set aside.

5 Layer the potato in the pastry shell, in an overlapping pattern, with the onion, gently pushing the layers in to compact them, finishing with onion. Combine the cream, egg and mustard, season and pour over the tart. Bake for 35 minutes, or until golden.

NUTRITION PER SERVE (6)
Protein 9 g; Fat 30 g; Carbohydrate 40 g;
Dietary Fibre 4 g; Cholesterol 155 mg;
2035 kJ (485 cal)

POTATO SALAD WITH HORSERADISH AND GARLIC DRESSING

Preparation time: 40 minutes
Total cooking time: 40 minutes
Serves 4–6

10 cloves garlic, unpeeled
2 tablespoons olive oil
8 potatoes, unpeeled
1/2 cup (125 g/4 oz) sour cream
3 teaspoons horseradish cream
1 teaspoon grated orange rind
2 tablespoons orange juice

1 tablespoon lemon juice
3 tablespoons chopped parsley
1 teaspoon soft brown sugar
30 g (1 oz) butter
1 large or 2 small leeks, sliced

1 Preheat the oven to moderate 180°C (350°F/Gas 4). Pierce each garlic clove with the tip of a sharp knife, put them on a baking tray, drizzle with olive oil and bake for 20 minutes, or until the garlic flesh is soft. Cool slightly.
2 Cut the potatoes into large chunks and boil or steam until tender. Drain and transfer to a large bowl.
3 Squeeze the garlic flesh from the

skins and put in a food processor with the sour cream, horseradish cream, orange rind and juice, lemon juice, parsley, sugar and salt and pepper, to taste. Process until smooth, then pour over the potato and toss.
4 Heat the butter in a large frying pan and, when foaming, add the sliced leek and lightly brown in the butter. Turn the slices over and brown the other side before arranging over the top of the potato salad.

NUTRITION PER SERVE (6)
Protein 7 g; Fat 20 g; Carbohydrate 30 g; Dietary Fibre 7 g; Cholesterol 40 mg; 1320 kJ (315 cal)

Pierce each garlic clove with the tip of a sharp knife before roasting.

Squeeze the garlic flesh out of the skins and place in a food processor.

Fry the leeks in butter, turning the slices to brown both sides.

JANSSON'S TEMPTATION

Preparation time: 15 minutes
Total cooking time: 1 hour 5 minutes
Serves 4

15 anchovy fillets
90 g (3 oz) butter
2 large onions, thinly sliced
5 potatoes, peeled and cut into julienne strips (the size and shape of matchsticks)
2 cups (500 ml/16 fl oz) cream

1 Preheat the oven to moderately hot 200°C (400°F/Gas 6). Soak the anchovies in water or milk for 5 minutes to lessen their saltiness. Rinse and drain.
2 Melt half the butter in a pan and cook the onion over medium heat for 5 minutes, or until golden. Chop the remaining butter into small cubes.
3 Spread half the potato over the base of a shallow ovenproof dish, top with the anchovies and onion and finish with the remaining potato.
4 Pour half the cream over the potato and scatter the butter cubes on top.

Bake for 20 minutes, or until golden. Pour the remaining cream over the top and cook for another 40 minutes, or until the potato is tender.

NUTRITION PER SERVE
Protein 11 g; Fat 70 g; Carbohydrate 30 g; Dietary Fibre 4 g; Cholesterol 240 mg; 3360 kJ (800 cal)

COOK'S FILE

Note: This Swedish dish is possibly named for the Swedish bass, Pelle Janzon (1844–1889) or perhaps after a 1929 film of the same name.

Soaking the anchovies in water, or milk, for a few minutes lessens the saltiness.

Spoon the anchovies and the fried onion over the layer of potato.

Pour half the cream over the dish, then top with the cubes of butter.

Potato salad with horseradish and garlic dressing (top) with Jansson's temptation

Baked Potatoes and Toppings

A PERFECT BAKED POTATO

Preheat the oven to hot 220°C (425°F/Gas 7). Wash and pat dry a large brushed potato. Prick on all sides gently with a fork and set on a baking tray. Lightly brush the potato with olive oil and bake for 1–1¹/2 hrs, or until tender when tested with a skewer. Remove from the tray and cut a deep cross in the top, creating a cavity. Fill with your selection of the following delicious toppings.

NUTRITION PER SERVE
Protein 3 g; Fat 5 g; Carbohydrate 15 g; Dietary Fibre 2 g; Cholesterol 0 mg; 350 kJ (85 cal)

Toppings

BACON AND MUSHROOMS WITH YOGHURT DRESSING

Combine some freshly chopped mint, parsley and chives in a bowl with a little natural yoghurt and mix together gently. Spoon into the cavity of a baked potato with some fried, sliced button mushrooms and crispy bacon.

NUTRITION PER SERVE
Protein 8 g; Fat 15 g; Carbohydrate 20 g; Dietary Fibre 3 g; Cholesterol 20 mg; 1015 kJ (240 cal)

Clockwise, from bottom left: Bacon and mushrooms with yoghurt dressing; Ratatouille topping; Plain baked potato; Hummus and tabouli; Blue cheese and caramelized onions; Chilli con carne with guacamole; Sour cream and sweet chilli sauce.

SOUR CREAM AND SWEET CHILLI SAUCE

Spoon a tablespoon of sour cream into the top of a baked potato. Top the potato with 1 teaspoon of Thai sweet chilli sauce and garnish with finely chopped chives. Serve immediately.

NUTRITION PER SERVE
Protein 4 g; Fat 10 g; Carbohydrate 25 g; Dietary Fibre 2 g; Cholesterol 25 mg; 820 kJ (195 cal)

CHILLI CON CARNE WITH GUACAMOLE

Fill a baked potato with leftover chilli con carne and top with guacamole and sour cream. Garnish with fresh chopped chives.

NUTRITION PER SERVE
Protein 6 g; Fat 10 g; Carbohydrate 15 g; Dietary Fibre 3 g; Cholesterol 20 mg; 670 kJ (160 cal)

BLUE CHEESE AND CARAMELIZED ONIONS

Fry a finely sliced onion in butter until it is well browned and caramelized. Tip the onion and any leftover butter into a baked potato and add some cubed blue cheese. Return the potato to the oven until the cheese has melted over the caramelized onions.

NUTRITION PER SERVE
Protein 10 g; Fat 25 g; Carbohydrate 20 g; Dietary Fibre 3 g; Cholesterol 65 mg; 1345 kJ (320 cal)

HUMMUS AND TABOULI

Put a spoonful of hummus into a baked potato and top with tabouli. For an extra creamy potato, add a spoonful of sour cream as well.

NUTRITION PER SERVE
Protein 7 g; Fat 15 g; Carbohydrate 25 g; Dietary Fibre 5 g; Cholesterol 25 mg; 1015 kJ (240 cal)

RATATOUILLE

Heat some ratatouille in a pan and spoon into a baked potato. Top with freshly grated Parmesan.

NUTRITION PER SERVE
Protein 5 g; Fat 5 g; Carbohydrate 15 g; Dietary Fibre 2 g; Cholesterol 5 mg; 460 kJ (110 cal)

TUNA AND MIXED BEANS

Thoroughly drain a small can of tuna and mix with a jar of antipasto-style mixed beans. Add some chopped fresh parsley and a squeeze of lemon juice. Spoon into a baked potato with a little olive oil.

NUTRITION PER SERVE
Protein 25 g; Fat 7 g; Carbohydrate 20 g; Dietary Fibre 4 g; Cholesterol 40 mg; 840 kJ (200 cal)

PRAWNS WITH GARLIC AND YOGHURT

Toss a handful of peeled cooked prawns in a hot pan with a little olive oil and a crushed clove of garlic. Add some chopped fresh chives and a small amount of natural yoghurt, stir well and season with salt and pepper, to taste. Spoon into a baked potato.

NUTRITION PER SERVE
Protein 15 g; Fat 6 g; Carbohydrate 15 g; Dietary Fibre 3 g; Cholesterol 70 mg; 570 kJ (135 cal)

MUSHROOM, GARLIC AND PARSLEY

Fry some thinly sliced mushrooms in olive oil with a clove of crushed garlic and a little chopped fresh parsley. Season, to taste, and serve in a potato, topped with a teaspoonful of sour cream.

NUTRITION PER SERVE
Protein 4 g; Fat 25 g; Carbohydrate 15 g; Dietary Fibre 3 g; Cholesterol 0 mg; 1060 kJ (255 cal)

GREEK-STYLE TOMATO WITH YOGHURT

Finely chop a tomato and add to some Greek-style yoghurt with grated cucumber, chopped mint and a finely chopped spring onion. Combine well and season with salt and pepper. Add a little cayenne pepper for a kick if you wish.

NUTRITION PER SERVE
Protein 4 g; Fat 5 g; Carbohydrate 20 g; Dietary Fibre 3 g; Cholesterol 3 mg; 430 kJ (100 cal)

CAULIFLOWER, BACON AND MUSTARD

Toss some small leftover cooked cauliflower florets in a pan with some chopped bacon or pastrami, until heated through and lightly browned. Mix a little wholegrain mustard and sour cream together, spoon into a baked potato and top with the cauliflower and meat.

NUTRITION PER SERVE
Protein 10 g; Fat 15 g; Carbohydrate 20 g; Dietary Fibre 3 g; Cholesterol 45 mg; 850 kJ (200 cal)

GUACAMOLE AND SOUR CREAM

Spoon some sour cream into a baked potato and top with a large spoonful of guacamole. Sprinkle with a little grated cheese.

NUTRITION PER SERVE
Protein 4 g; Fat 15 g; Carbohydrate 15 g; Dietary Fibre 2 g; Cholesterol 27 mg; 775 kJ (185 cal)

HERB CHEESE AND PINE NUT

Fill a baked potato with a large spoonful of herbed cream cheese and put back into the oven for a couple of minutes. Meanwhile, toast a few pine nuts and when the cream cheese has melted, scatter with pine nuts.

NUTRITION PER SERVE
Protein 6 g; Fat 15 g; Carbohydrate 15 g; Dietary Fibre 2 g; Cholesterol 20 mg; 810 kJ (195 cal)

SWEET CORN SALSA

Drain a small can of sweet corn and combine with a chopped tomato, a finely sliced spring onion, 1/2 chopped chilli, and some chopped fresh coriander. Add a tablespoon of olive oil and a squeeze of lemon juice. Spoon into a potato.

NUTRITION PER SERVE
Protein 6 g; Fat 25 g; Carbohydrate 30 g; Dietary Fibre 6 g; Cholesterol 0 mg; 1425 kJ (340 cal)

BROCCOLI SOUFFLE

Roughly purée some leftover broccoli with a little sour cream and some cheese until you have a thick paste, add a beaten egg and mix well. Spoon a little potato out of the top of a baked potato and replace with the mixture. Return the potato to a hot oven and cook until the filling has risen and is golden brown on top.

NUTRITION PER SERVE
Protein 15 g; Fat 20 g; Carbohydrate 15 g; Dietary Fibre 4 g; Cholesterol 220 mg; 1205 kJ (290 cal)

Top to bottom, left: Tuna and mixed beans; Prawns with garlic and yoghurt; Mushroom, garlic and parsley; Greek-style tomato and yoghurt; Middle: Cauliflower, bacon and mustard; Guacamole and sour cream; Herb cheese and pine nut; Right: Plain baked potato; Sweet corn salsa; Broccoli soufflé.

POTATO AND CHICKPEA PANCAKES

Preparation time: 30 minutes
  + 30 minutes resting
Total cooking time: 20 minutes
Serves 4

600 g (1¹/₄ lb) waxy potatoes
1 small onion
3 tablespoons chopped
    coriander
2 spring onions, finely sliced,
    some green part included
4 tablespoons besan (chickpea
    flour)
2 teaspoons harissa
³/₄ teaspoon salt
¹/₄ teaspoon freshly ground
    black pepper
pinch of cayenne pepper
1 egg, beaten
vegetable oil, for frying
1 teaspoon ground coriander
¹/₄ teaspoon ground turmeric
³/₄ teaspoon cumin seeds

1 Grate the potatoes and onion, place in a bowl and cover with cold water.
2 Put the fresh coriander, spring onion, besan, harissa, salt, pepper and cayenne into another bowl. Mix together and stir in the egg. Heat 2 tablespoons of oil in a large non-stick frying pan and fry the ground coriander, turmeric and cumin seeds over medium-high heat, stirring, for 25–30 seconds. Add to the bowl.
3 Drain the potato and onion and wring out in a tea towel to extract the liquid. Add to the other ingredients and mix together with your hands. Cover and set aside for 30 minutes. Wipe out the frying pan with paper towel and preheat the oven to very slow 120°C (250°F/Gas ¹/₂).
4 Heat 1–2 tablespoons of the oil in the frying pan. Spoon a heaped tablespoon of potato mixture into the pan and flatten to a rough circle, using a metal spatula. Cook for 2–3 minutes on each side, or until golden. The pancakes are a little fragile until cooked on both sides, so take care when flipping them over. Transfer to an ovenproof plate and keep warm in the oven while cooking the rest of the pancakes, in batches, adding more oil to the pan as needed.

NUTRITION PER SERVE
Protein 10 g; Fat 15 g; Carbohydrate 30 g; Dietary Fibre 6 g; Cholesterol 45 mg; 1315 kJ (315 cal)

Grate the potato and onion and soak in cold water to remove the starch.

COOK'S FILE

Note: Harissa is usually available from large supermarkets, otherwise try speciality shops.

Use about a heaped tablespoonful of mixture to make each pancake.

POTATO CHEDDAR SOUP

Preparation time: 15 minutes + cooling
Total cooking time: 30 minutes
Serves 4–6

50 g (1³/4 oz) butter
2 onions, chopped
750 g (1¹/2 lb) floury potatoes,
    peeled and chopped
3 cups (750 ml/24 fl oz) chicken
    stock
1¹/2 cups (375 ml/12 fl oz) milk

1¹/2 cups (185 g/6 oz) grated
    vintage Cheddar cheese
cayenne pepper, to taste
2 tablespoons chopped walnuts
1 small celery stick, chopped
1 tablespoon chopped chives

1 Melt the butter in a large pan, add the onion and cook until soft but not brown. Add the potato and stock, bring to the boil, reduce the heat, cover and simmer for 20 minutes or until the potato is cooked. Leave to cool for 10–15 minutes.

2 Process the soup, in batches, in a blender, until smooth. Return to the rinsed pan, add the milk and bring to the boil, stirring occasionally. Remove from the heat, add the cheese and stir until the cheese is melted. Season with salt and cayenne pepper, to taste. Cover and keep hot but do not boil.
3 Mix the walnuts, celery and chives. Sprinkle on the soup to serve.

NUTRITION PER SERVE (6)
Protein 15 g; Fat 25 g; Carbohydrate 20 g; Dietary Fibre 3 g; Cholesterol 60 mg; 1535 kJ (365 cal)

Fry the onion until soft, then add the potato and stock.

Purée the soup in batches, return to the pan and add the milk.

Remove the soup from the heat before stirring in the grated cheese.

TWO-TONED POTATO GNOCCHI

Preparation time: 1 hour 30 minutes
Total cooking time: 45 minutes
Serves 4–6

450 g (14 oz) floury potatoes,
    peeled and chopped
200 g (6½ oz) orange sweet
    potato, peeled and chopped
1½ cups (185 g/6 oz) plain flour
Parmesan shavings, to garnish

Tomato and coriander sauce
2 tablespoons olive oil
3 cloves garlic, sliced thickly
1 onion, chopped
1 kg (2 lb) ripe tomatoes, peeled
    and chopped
1 small red chilli, seeded and
    finely chopped
⅓ cup (10 g/⅓ oz) coriander
    leaves

1 Steam or boil the chopped potato and sweet potato until tender and mash them in separate bowls. Add 1 cup (125 g/4 oz) of flour, with 1 teaspoon of salt to the plain potato and bring together to make a smooth dough. Add enough of the remaining flour to the sweet potato to gently bring together. The mixtures should be slightly sticky to touch. On a lightly floured surface, press the two doughs together gently until they have a two-tone appearance.

2 Divide the mixture into four and roll each, on a lightly floured surface, into a log about 2.5 cm (1 inch) thick. Slice the logs into 2 cm (3/4 inch) pieces. Shape each piece into ovals and roll the gnocchi ovals onto the prongs of a floured fork. You should have about 40 pieces. Put on a lightly floured tray and cover.

3 To make the tomato and coriander sauce, heat the oil in a heavy-based pan, add the garlic and cook over low heat for 2 minutes, or until it just begins to brown slightly. Remove with a slotted spoon and discard. Add the onion and cook until softened. Add the tomato and bring to the boil. Reduce the heat and simmer for 30–35 minutes, stirring occasionally. Add the chilli and coriander leaves. Season, to taste.

4 Lower the gnocchi into boiling water, in batches, and cook for 2 minutes, or until they float to the surface. Remove each batch with a slotted spoon. Serve on the sauce.

Garnish with the Parmesan shavings.

NUTRITION PER SERVE (6)
Protein 7 g; Fat 7 g; Carbohydrate 40 g;
Dietary Fibre 4 g; Cholesterol 2 mg;
1060 kJ (255 cal)

Press the two doughs together gently until they take on a two-tone appearance.

Roll the gnocchi over the back of a fork to give the characteristic indentations.

POTATO FILO PARCELS

Preparation time: 1 hour
Total cooking time: 1 hour 20 minutes
Serves 6

6 Roma tomatoes, halved
    lengthways
3 tablespoons olive oil
50 g (1³/4 oz) butter
3 cloves garlic, crushed
800 g (1 lb 10 oz) potatoes,
    unpeeled and sliced
500 g (1 lb) English spinach,
    trimmed
12 sheets filo pastry
100 g (3¹/2 oz) butter, melted
2 tablespoons sesame seeds

1 Preheat the oven to moderately hot 200°C (400°F/Gas 6). Place the tomato halves, cut-side-up, on a baking tray, drizzle with 1 tablespoon of the oil and sprinkle with 1 teaspoon of salt. Bake for 40 minutes.
2 Heat the butter and remaining oil in a large non-stick pan. Add the garlic and potato and cook over medium heat, tossing occasionally, for 10 minutes, or until the potato is tender. Set aside on paper towels. Cook the spinach in the pan for 1–2 minutes, or until wilted. Cool and then squeeze out any excess moisture.
3 Reduce the oven to moderate 180°C (350°F/Gas 4). Work with one sheet of pastry at a time and cover the rest with a damp tea towel. Brush the

pastry with melted butter and place another sheet on top. Brush with butter and repeat with another two layers. Cut in half widthways. Place a few potato slices at one end of each half, leaving a wide border on each side. Top with two tomato pieces and some spinach. Season. Fold in the sides of the pastry and roll up. Place on a lightly greased baking tray, brush with melted butter and sprinkle with sesame seeds. Use the remaining filo and filling to make another five parcels. Bake for 25–30 minutes, or until lightly golden.

NUTRITION PER SERVE
Protein 9 g; Fat 30 g; Carbohydrate 35 g; Dietary Fibre 6 g; Cholesterol 60 mg; 1940 kJ (465 cal)

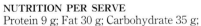

Build up the layers of filo pastry, brushing each with melted butter.

Place a few slices of potato at one end and top with tomato and spinach.

Fold in the sides of the pastry and then roll up around the filling, into a parcel.

BRILLIANT IDEAS

SCALLOPS IN COGNAC CREAM ON A BED OF SOFT STRAW POTATO

Preparation time: 40 minutes
Total cooking time: 15–20 minutes
Serves 6

500 g (1 lb) potatoes, peeled
500 g (1 lb) orange sweet
    potato, peeled
1 kg (2 lb) scallops
50 g (1³/4 oz) butter
2³/4 cups (340 g/10³/4 oz) sliced
    spring onions
2 cloves garlic, crushed
¹/2 cup (125 ml/4 fl oz) cream
1 tablespoon cognac
2 eggs, beaten
4 tablespoons plain flour
vegetable oil, for frying

1 Slice the potatoes and sweet potato into long thin sticks. Set aside.
2 Remove the vein and muscles from the scallops and rinse gently. Pat dry and return to the refrigerator.
3 Melt the butter in a heavy-based pan and cook the spring onion for 5 minutes over medium heat, stirring. Add the garlic and continue cooking until the spring onion is soft. Remove from the pan. In the same pan, sear the scallops in small batches for 1–2 minutes over medium-high heat. Drain off any excess liquid.
4 Return the spring onion to the pan, and over high heat stir through the cream and cognac for 1–2 minutes. Season, to taste. Bring to the boil, reduce the heat and simmer over low heat for 2–3 minutes. Return the scallops to the pan. Keep warm.
5 Combine the eggs and flour in a large bowl, add the potato and toss until well coated. In a separate heavy-based pan, heat the oil for shallow-frying to 180°C/350°F (a cube of bread dropped into the oil will brown in 15 seconds).
6 Lower small batches of the potato into the oil and cook over medium heat until golden. The potato straw beds should be roughly knitted together, but not too crisp. Drain on paper towels.
7 To serve, lay a portion of potato straws on individual plates and season with salt and pepper. Spoon the scallops and cream on top and serve.

NUTRITION PER SERVE
Protein 45 g; Fat 30 g; Carbohydrate 30 g; Dietary Fibre 5 g; Cholesterol 210 mg; 2415 kJ (575 cal)

Before rinsing the scallops, pull away the vein and muscles.

Use tongs to lower small batches of the potato sticks into the hot oil.

SUMMER POTATO PIZZA

Preparation time: 30 minutes
Total cooking time: 40 minutes
Serves 4–6

7 g (¹/4 oz) sachet dry yeast
2¹/2 cups (310 g/10 oz) plain flour
2 teaspoons polenta or semolina
3 tablespoons olive oil
2 cloves garlic, crushed
4–5 potatoes, unpeeled and
**   thinly sliced**
1 tablespoon rosemary leaves

1 Preheat the oven to hot 210°C (415°F/Gas 6–7). Combine the yeast, ¹/2 teaspoon of salt and sugar and 1 cup (250 ml/8 fl oz) of warm water in a bowl. Cover and leave in a warm place for 10 minutes, or until foamy. Sift the flour into a bowl, make a well in the centre, add the yeast mixture and mix to a dough.

2 Turn the dough out onto a lightly floured surface and knead for 5 minutes, or until smooth and elastic. Roll out to a 30 cm (12 inch) circle. Lightly brush a pizza tray with oil and sprinkle with polenta or semolina.

3 Place the pizza base on the tray. Mix 1 tablespoon of the oil with the garlic and brush over the pizza base. Gently toss the remaining olive oil, potato slices, rosemary leaves, 1 teaspoon of salt and some freshly cracked black pepper in a bowl.

4 Arrange the potato slices in overlapping circles over the pizza base and bake for 40 minutes, or until the base is crisp and golden.

NUTRITION PER SERVE (6)
Protein 9 g; Fat 10 g; Carbohydrate 50 g; Dietary Fibre 4 g; Cholesterol 0 mg; 1415 kJ (340 cal)

Leave the yeast mixture in a warm place until it is foamy.

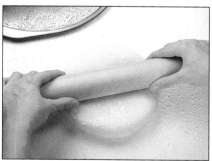

Knead the dough until firm and elastic, then roll out to fit a pizza tray.

Brush the dough base with garlic oil, then top with a layer of potato slices.

RED HOT POTATO SALAD

Preparation time: 25 minutes
Total cooking time: 20 minutes
Serves 4–6

3 rashers bacon, rind removed
5 potatoes, unpeeled and cut
   into chunks
3 spring onions, sliced
2 sticks celery, sliced
1 small red onion, sliced
2 tablespoons lemon thyme leaves
2 tablespoons chopped parsley

Dressing
$1/3$ cup (90 g/3 oz) sour cream
$1/4$ cup (60 g/2 oz) whole egg
   mayonnaise
1 tablespoon Dijon mustard
1 tablespoon lemon juice
Tabasco

1 Cut the bacon into thin strips and cook in a non-stick frying pan, over medium heat, until browned and crisp. Remove from the pan and drain on paper towels. Boil or steam the potato until just tender. Drain well.
2 Combine the spring onion, celery, onion, lemon thyme leaves and parsley with the drained potato and bacon in a large bowl.
3 Mix together all the dressing ingredients, adding drops of Tabasco (add a drop at a time—it is very fiery) and seasoning with salt and pepper, to taste. Pour the dressing over the salad and toss gently until the salad is completely coated. Serve hot or at room temperature.

NUTRITION PER SERVE (6)
Protein 7 g; Fat 10 g; Carbohydrate 15 g; Dietary Fibre 2 g; Cholesterol 30 mg; 795 kJ (190 cal)

Cut the bacon into thin strips and cook in a non-stick pan until crisp.

Cook the potato pieces until they are tender to the point of a knife.

Mix together the potato and other salad ingredients before adding the dressing.

POTATO PATTIES

Preparation time: 1 hour
 + 1 hour refrigeration
Total cooking time: 30 minutes
Serves 8–10

500 g (1 lb) purple congo
 potatoes or sweet potatoes,
 peeled
30 g (1 oz) butter
6 spring onions, finely chopped
1/4 teaspoon ground allspice
1/4 teaspoon garam masala
1 egg yolk
300 g (10 oz) flaked almonds,
 toasted
1/4 cup (25 g/3/4 oz) dry
 breadcrumbs
2 eggs
1/2 cup (60 g/2 oz) plain flour
300 g (10 oz) goats cheese, at
 room temperature
1 tablespoon cream
vegetable oil, for shallow-frying

1 Boil or steam the potato until tender and drain. Melt the butter in a heavy-based pan and cook the spring onion over low heat until soft. Mash the hot potato with the spring onion, spices and salt and pepper, to taste. Mix in the egg yolk. Form into patties, using 1 tablespoon of mash for each. Put on a paper-lined tray, cover and refrigerate for 30 minutes.

2 Chop the almonds in a food processor for 2–3 seconds. Mix with the breadcrumbs and put on a plate.

3 Beat the eggs and slowly add the flour and 100 ml (3 1/2 fl oz) of water while whisking. Mash the goats cheese and cream together.

4 Slice the cold potato patties in half horizontally. Put 2 teaspoons of the goats cheese onto one half and spread to the edge. Replace the top half and re-form the patty.

5 Dip the patties into the egg mixture and roll in the almond crumbs. Cover and chill for 30 minutes. Heat 1 cm (1/2 inch) of oil in a pan and fry the patties, in batches, for 30 seconds each side, or until golden brown. Drain on paper towels and serve hot.

NUTRITION PER SERVE (10)
Protein 15 g; Fat 35 g; Carbohydrate 15 g;
Dietary Fibre 4 g; Cholesterol 95 mg;
1920 kJ (460 cal)

Purple congo potatoes have a strange colouring but can be cooked as usual.

Chop the almonds in a food processor for a couple of seconds.

Chill the patties well, as this will make them much easier to slice in half.

Coat the patties in egg and almond crumbs, then fry in batches.

POTATO PETALS WITH GREEN SALAD

Preparation time: 30 minutes
Total cooking time: 5–10 minutes
Serves 4

2 new potatoes, unpeeled
1 clove garlic
1/4 cup (60 ml/2 fl oz) walnut oil
1 tablespoon red wine vinegar
1/2 teaspoon grated fresh ginger

1 teaspoon Dijon mustard
150 g (5 oz) rocket
1 avocado, sliced
8 cherry tomatoes, cut in halves

1 Slice the potatoes paper-thin, using a sharp knife or a mandolin. Cut the garlic in half and rub the cut side over each slice of potato. Put the potato slices on paper towels to dry.
2 Put the oil, vinegar, ginger and mustard in a screw top jar and shake well. Season with salt and pepper and then toss together with the rocket.
3 Half fill a pan with oil and heat to 180°C/350°F (a cube of bread will brown in 15 seconds). Deep-fry the potato petals a few at a time until crisp. Drain on paper towels and sprinkle with salt. Serve some avocado, tomato and warm potato petals over each salad serving.

NUTRITION PER SERVE
Protein 3 g; Fat 30 g; Carbohydrate 9 g;
Dietary Fibre 3 g; Cholesterol 0 mg;
1260 kJ (300 cal)

If you have one, use a mandolin to slice the potatoes thinly.

Rub the cut side of the garlic clove over the potato slices.

Drain the potato petals on paper towels after frying, and sprinkle with salt.

CAMEMBERT AND POTATO TERRINE

Preparation time: 1 hour
+ overnight refrigeration
Total cooking time: 55 minutes
Serves 8–10

6 new potatoes, unpeeled
3 medium Granny Smith apples
125 g (4 oz) butter
3 tablespoons olive oil
200 g (6½ oz) Camembert,
    chilled and very thinly sliced
2 tablespoons chopped parsley

1 Parboil the potatoes in salted water for about 15 minutes. Drain and cool, then peel and cut into slices 1 cm (½ inch) thick. Core and slice the apples into 5 mm (¼ inch) thick rounds. Heat half the butter and half the oil in a pan and cook the potato until just golden. Drain on paper towels. Heat the remaining butter and oil. Lightly sauté the apple until golden and drain on paper towels.

2 Line a 6-cup terrine with baking paper. Preheat the oven to moderate 180°C (350°F/Gas 4).

3 Arrange a layer of potato neatly in the base of the terrine. Add a layer of apple and then Camembert. Sprinkle with parsley and season with salt and pepper, to taste. Build up the layers, finishing with potato.

4 Oil a piece of foil and cover the terrine, sealing well. Place the terrine in a baking dish and half fill the dish with water. Bake for 20 minutes. Remove from the oven and place a weight, such as a can, directly on top of the terrine. Chill overnight. Turn out and slice, to serve.

NUTRITION PER SERVE (10)
Protein 6 g; Fat 15 g; Carbohydrate 15 g; Dietary Fibre 2 g; Cholesterol 50 mg; 935 kJ (225 cal)

Core and slice the apples, then sauté in oil and butter until golden.

Build up the layers of potato, apple and cheese, seasoning with salt and pepper.

Weigh the terrine down to compress the layers, chill and turn out to serve.

Pierce the potatoes a few times with a skewer before baking.

Scoop out the cooked potato, leaving enough in the skin to form a firm shell.

Carefully fold the beaten egg white into the potato filling.

SOUFFLE POTATOES

Preparation time: 25 minutes
Total cooking time: 1 hour 20 minutes
Makes 4

**4 large floury potatoes,
    unpeeled
1/2 cup (60 g/2 oz) grated
    Cheddar cheese
2 tablespoons sour cream
3 eggs, separated
1 spring onion, finely chopped
1 tablespoon chopped parsley**

1 Preheat the oven to moderate 180°C (350°F/Gas 4). Pierce the potatoes two or three times with a skewer. Bake for 50 minutes, or until cooked through when tested with a skewer. Increase the oven temperature to moderately hot 200°C (400°F/Gas 6).

2 Cut the top off each potato and discard. Carefully scoop out the potato flesh, leaving enough attached to the skin to make a firm shell. Mash the potato in the bowl and mix in the Cheddar cheese, sour cream, egg yolks, spring onion and parsley. Season, to taste.

3 Using a clean bowl and beaters, beat the egg whites until firm peaks form. Gently fold a quarter of the egg white into the potato mixture to loosen it up, then carefully fold in the remainder. Pile the mixture into the potato shells, place on a baking tray and bake for 30 minutes, or until puffed and golden. Serve at once.

Spoon the soufflé filling into the potato shells and bake until puffed and golden.

NUTRITION PER SERVE
Protein 15 g; Fat 15 g; Carbohydrate 15 g; Dietary Fibre 2 g; Cholesterol 160 mg; 1000 kJ (240 cal)

95

Purées and Mash

The best potatoes for mashing are floury ones. Use a masher, mouli or potato ricer, but do not put them in a food processor or they will go gluey. Always drain the cooked potato thoroughly. To remove all excess moisture, you can return the drained potato to the pan and heat briefly before mashing.

POTATO AND CELERIAC PUREE

Add the juice of 1 lemon to a large bowl of water. Peel and cut 1 kg (2 lb) of celeriac into cubes and put them in the water immediately, to prevent browning. Peel and cube 500 g (1 lb) of potatoes. Boil the celeriac and potato in separate saucepans until soft. Drain both and return the potato to its pan with 50 g (1¾ oz) butter, 2 tablespoons of cream and 3 tablespoons of chopped parsley. Mash until smooth and fluffy. Process the celeriac in a food processor and beat it into the potato with salt and pepper, to taste. Serves 4–6.

NUTRITION PER SERVE (6)
Protein 5 g; Fat 10 g; Carbohydrate 20 g; Dietary Fibre 9 g; Cholesterol 30 mg; 805 kJ (190 cal)

TWICE-COOKED POTATO PUREE

Halve, seed and quarter 2 small capsicums, one red and one green, grill skin-side-up until blackened, cool, peel and chop. Boil 4 large peeled potatoes until soft, drain and put in a bowl. Mash until smooth and add the capsicum, 30 g (1 oz) butter, 4 tablespoons chopped parsley and salt and pepper. Refrigerate until firm and, using ¼ cup of potato for each, make 10 patties about 1.5 cm (⅝ inch) thick. Refrigerate for another 30 minutes, then coat each with flour and fry for 2–3 minutes each side in 1 cm (½ inch) of oil. Drain on paper towels and serve hot. Serves 4–6.

NUTRITION PER SERVE (6)
Protein 3 g; Fat 8 g; Carbohydrate 15 g; Dietary Fibre 2 g; Cholesterol 8 mg; 640 kJ (155 cal)

From top left: Potato and celeriac purée; Twice-cooked potato purée; Colcannon.

COLCANNON

Peel and quarter 4 large potatoes. Boil until soft, drain, return to the pan and mash well with 50 g (1³/4 oz) of butter and ²/3 cup (170 ml/5¹/2 fl oz) milk. Stir-fry 3 cups (200 g/6¹/2 oz) finely shredded green cabbage in 30 g (1 oz) of butter until softened and slightly browned. Add 8 finely chopped spring onions. Add to the potato and season with salt, pepper and nutmeg. Sprinkle with 1 tablespoon of finely chopped parsley before serving. Serves 4.

NUTRITION PER SERVE
Protein 9 g; Fat 20 g; Carbohydrate 40 g; Dietary Fibre 7 g; Cholesterol 60 mg; 1490 kJ (355 cal)

POTATO AND PARSNIP MASH

Peel and chop 2 large potatoes and 5 large parsnips, discarding any woody centres from the parsnips, and boil until soft. Drain the vegetables and transfer to a large bowl. Add 30 g (1 oz) butter, 1 tablespoon of milk and 2 tablespoons of sour cream and mash until smooth and fluffy. Season generously with salt and pepper. Serve at once. Serves 4–6.

NUTRITION PER SERVE (6)
Protein 5 g; Fat 7 g; Carbohydrate 25 g; Dietary Fibre 5 g; Cholesterol 20 mg; 795 kJ (190 cal)

CHEESY HERB MASH

Peel and quarter 4 large potatoes and boil until soft. Drain, return to the pan and mix in ¹/2 cup (60 g/2 oz) of grated vintage Cheddar cheese, 3 tablespoons of grated Parmesan and 3 tablespoons of cream. Mash until fluffy. Stir through 2 tablespoons each of snipped chives and chopped flat-leaf parsley and season well with salt and pepper, to taste. Serves 4.

NUTRITION PER SERVE
Protein 15 g; Fat 15 g; Carbohydrate 35 g; Dietary Fibre 4 g; Cholesterol 45 mg; 1325 kJ (315 cal)

OLIVE MASH

Peel and chop 4 large potatoes and boil until soft. Meanwhile, cook 1 crushed or chopped clove of garlic in a small pan with ¹/4 cup (60 ml/2 fl oz) of olive oil until golden and slightly softened. Drain the potato thoroughly, return to the pan and mash until fluffy. Mix in the oil and garlic as well as ¹/4 cup (35 g/1¹/4 oz) of chopped lemon-chilli marinated olives. Season with salt and pepper, to taste. Serves 4.

NUTRITION PER SERVE
Protein 6 g; Fat 15 g; Carbohydrate 30 g; Dietary Fibre 4 g; Cholesterol 0 mg; 1235 kJ (295 cal)

From bottom left: Potato and parsnip mash; Cheesy herb mash; Olive mash.

POTATO AND OLIVE PASTRIES WITH CAPSICUM COULIS

Preparation time: 40 minutes
Total cooking time: 55 minutes
Serves 4

2 sheets ready-rolled frozen
    puff pastry
300 g (10 oz) floury potatoes,
    peeled
1 kg (2 lb) yellow capsicums
250 g (8 oz) zucchini, sliced
    lengthways
1 tablespoon olive oil
1 tablespoon chopped basil
    leaves
1 egg, beaten
olive tapenade, to serve
100 g (3½ oz) semi-dried
    tomatoes

1 Defrost the puff pastry sheets. Cook the potato in boiling water until tender. Slice the capsicums in half, discarding the seeds and membrane, and place, skin-side-up, under a hot grill until the skin is blistered and blackened. Leave to cool under a damp tea towel, then peel away the skin and purée the flesh in a food processor until smooth. Drain the potato and mash with 2 tablespoons of the yellow capsicum. Keep warm.

2 In a bowl, mix the zucchini with the oil and chopped fresh basil and then set aside for 15 minutes. Season, then grill on a lined baking tray until both sides are golden. Keep warm.

3 Preheat the oven to moderately hot 200°C (400°F/Gas 6). Cut the pastry sheets into quarters and put on a lined tray. Prick all over with a fork. Brush with egg and bake for 10–15 minutes, or until puffed and golden.

4 To assemble, spread a thin layer of tapenade over four of the pastry squares, and then spread the potato mash on top of that. Top with pieces of semi-dried tomato and then the zucchini, finishing with another pastry square. Serve with the remaining yellow capsicum coulis and olive tapenade.

NUTRITION PER SERVE
Protein 15 g; Fat 25 g; Carbohydrate 45 g; Dietary Fibre 6 g; Cholesterol 65 mg; 2135 kJ (505 cal)

Drain the potato and mash with a little of the puréed yellow capsicum.

Mix the zucchini with the oil and chopped basil, then grill until golden.

Brush the pastry squares with beaten egg and bake until puffed and golden.

Spread the pastry with tapenade and potato mash, then tomato and zucchini.

POTATO AND ROCKET SOUP

Preparation time: 15 minutes
Total cooking time: 30 minutes
Serves 4

1 onion, chopped
2 celery sticks, finely chopped
1 clove garlic, crushed
600 g (1¼ lb) floury potatoes,
    peeled and chopped
4 cups (1 litre) chicken stock
2 cups (90 g/3 oz) rocket
    leaves, roughly chopped
½ cup (125 ml/4 fl oz) cream
grated Parmesan, to garnish

1 Heat a little olive oil in a large pan and cook the onion, celery and garlic until soft but not brown. Add the chopped potato and half the chicken stock and bring slowly to the boil. Reduce the heat and simmer, covered, until the potato is cooked. Cool for 10 minutes, then add the rocket. Process the soup, in batches, in a blender, until smooth.
2 Return to the rinsed pan, add the remaining stock and bring to the boil.
3 Stir in the cream and season, to taste, with salt and ground pepper. Reheat the soup without boiling. Serve sprinkled with Parmesan.

NUTRITION PER SERVE
Protein 7 g; Fat 15 g; Carbohydrate 20 g;
Dietary Fibre 4 g; Cholesterol 45 mg;
1080 kJ (260 cal)

Cook the onion, celery and garlic until soft but not browned.

Add the potato and half the chicken stock and bring slowly to the boil

Cool the soup for 10 minutes and then add the rocket.

EGGPLANT ROLLS FILLED WITH POTATO, TOMATO AND BABY SPINACH

Preparation time: 45 minutes
 + 1 hour resting
Total cooking time: 1 hour 15 minutes
Serves 4–6

2 large eggplant, about 350 g
    (11 oz) each
450 g (14 oz) waxy potatoes,
    peeled
1 tomato
3 tablespoons olive oil
2 tablespoons sultanas
2 tablespoons pine nuts
2 cloves garlic, crushed
1½ cups (about 100 g/3½ oz)
    firmly packed, shredded
    English spinach leaves
¼ teaspoon cayenne pepper, or
    to taste
pinch of nutmeg
2 tablespoons chopped
    coriander
1 spring onion, finely chopped
2 bay leaves
3 tablespoons grated Parmesan
    or Pecorino cheese

1 Slice the eggplant lengthways into 5 mm (¼ inch) slices and spread out on paper towels. Sprinkle with salt and leave to drain for 1 hour.
2 Cook the potato in plenty of salted boiling water until just tender.
3 Score a cross in the base of the tomato, pierce it in the top with a fork, then submerge it in the boiling potato water for 10 seconds. Plunge into cold water, then peel the skin away from the cross. Cut the tomato in half, remove the stem and scoop out the seeds. Dice the flesh and put in a bowl. Drain the potatoes, rinse under cold water, then cut into small cubes. (It's not a problem if they look a little mashed.) Add to the tomato.
4 Heat half the olive oil in a pan and add the sultanas and pine nuts. Sauté over medium heat until the sultanas are puffed and the pine nuts golden, then add the garlic and spinach. Cook, stirring, for 1–2 minutes, or until the spinach wilts. Remove from the heat and add to the tomato and potato, including the oil from the pan. Toss to combine. Add the cayenne, nutmeg, coriander and spring onion and season well with salt and freshly ground black pepper.
5 Preheat the oven to moderate 180°C (350°F/Gas 4). Bring a large pan of water to the boil. Pat the eggplant slices dry with paper towels and blanch in the water for 3–4 minutes, or until soft. Put a tablespoon of the potato filling on each eggplant slice, then roll it up tightly. You may need a wooden skewer to prevent it unrolling. If the eggplant slices are too small to roll successfully, just fold them over once to enclose the filling.
6 Arrange the rolls in a single layer in a greased ovenproof dish. Brush the remaining oil over the top, add the bay leaves and sprinkle with Pecorino cheese. Bake for 15–20 minutes, or until golden and heated through.

NUTRITION PER SERVE (6)
Protein 10 g; Fat 20 g; Carbohydrate 15 g; Dietary Fibre 4 g; Cholesterol 20 mg; 1270 kJ (305 cal)

COOK'S FILE

Note: Rather than baking in the oven, this dish can be grilled if you prefer. You will need to omit the bay leaves, or they will burn.

Sprinkle the eggplant slices with salt and leave to drain for about 1 hour.

Peel the skin away from the cross before removing the seeds and dicing the flesh.

Drain the cooked potato and cut it into small cubes.

Blanch the eggplant slices in boiling water for 3–4 minutes.

Put 1 tablespoon of filling on each eggplant slice and roll up tightly.

Add the bay leaves and sprinkle the cheese over the rolls.

POTATO, GARLIC AND LIME DIP

Preparation time: 15 minutes
Total cooking time: 20–25 minutes
Serves 4–6

250 g (8 oz) potatoes, unpeeled
2 cloves garlic
1 1/2 tablespoons lime juice
150 ml (5 fl oz) cream

3 tablespoons sour cream
1/2 cup (125 ml/4 fl oz) light
  olive oil
pinch of cayenne pepper

1 Put the potatoes and garlic in a pan, cover with water and add a pinch of salt. Bring to the boil, reduce the heat and simmer until the potato is tender.
2 Drain, rinse, then peel the potatoes when cool enough to handle. Purée in a food processor with the garlic. Blend

in the lime juice, cream, sour cream and oil. Add the cayenne pepper and salt, to taste. Serve as a dip or with grilled meats, seafood or kebabs.

NUTRITION PER SERVE (6)
Protein 2 g; Fat 35 g; Carbohydrate 7 g; Dietary Fibre 0 g; Cholesterol 45 mg; 1425 kJ (340 cal)

COOK'S FILE

Hint: Thin with a little more cream and use to dress vegetables or salads.

Put the potato and peeled garlic cloves in a pan and cover with water.

Boil the potatoes until tender and then peel away the skins.

Purée the potatoes and garlic, then add the lime juice, cream, sour cream and oil.

POTATO NOODLE NIBBLIES

Preparation time: 30 minutes + cooling
Total cooking time: 40 minutes
Serves 4–6

450 g (14 oz) floury potatoes, peeled and chopped
40 g (1¼ oz) butter, softened
2 tablespoons grated Parmesan or Pecorino cheese
100 g (3½ oz) besan (chickpea flour)
2 teaspoons ground cumin
2 teaspoons garam masala
1 teaspoon ground coriander
1 teaspoon chilli powder
1 teaspoon cayenne pepper
1½ teaspoons ground turmeric
vegetable oil, for frying

1 Boil or steam the potato until tender. Drain and cool for 15–20 minutes, then mash with the butter and cheese. Add the besan, cumin, garam masala, coriander, chilli powder, cayenne, turmeric and ¾ teaspoon of salt and mix with a wooden spoon until a soft, light dough forms. Turn out and knead lightly 10–12 times, until smooth.

2 Fill a large pan with vegetable oil to a depth of at least 10 cm (4 inches) and heat to 190°C/375°F. Test the temperature by dropping a small ball of dough into the oil. It is ready if the dough rises immediately to the surface.

3 Using a piping bag with a 1 cm (½ inch) star nozzle, pipe short lengths of dough into the oil, in manageable batches. They will rise to the surface and turn golden quickly. Remove them with a slotted spoon and drain on paper towels. Serve within 2 hours, as a snack or to accompany drinks.

NUTRITION PER SERVE (6)
Protein 7 g; Fat 15 g; Carbohydrate 20 g; Dietary Fibre 4 g; Cholesterol 20 mg; 1050 kJ (250 cal)

Mash the cooled potato with the butter and cheese.

Turn out the dough and knead lightly to give a smooth texture.

Pipe short lengths of the dough into the hot oil.

POTATO AND GOATS CHEESE PIES

Preparation time: 25 minutes
Total cooking time: 1 hour
Makes 4

4 medium potatoes, peeled
150 g (5 oz) goats cheese
4 slices prosciutto
1 cup (250 g/8 oz) sour
    cream
2 eggs, lightly beaten
1/2 cup (125 ml/4 fl oz) cream

1 Brush four 1-cup (250 ml/8 fl oz) ramekins with melted butter. Preheat the oven to 180°C (350°F/Gas 4).
2 To assemble each pie, thinly slice a potato and pat the slices dry with paper towels. Cut the goats cheese into four evenly-sized pieces. Line the base of a ramekin with half a slice of prosciutto. Layer half the potato slices neatly into the dish. Put the other half slice of prosciutto on top and crumble a portion of the goats cheese over it. Cover with the remaining potato slices and press down firmly. The potato should fill the dish to the top.

3 Repeat this process with the remaining ramekins. Mix together the sour cream, eggs, cream and salt and pepper, to taste, and pour into each ramekin, allowing it to seep through. Place on a baking tray and bake for 50–60 minutes, or until the potato is cooked when tested with a skewer. Leave for 5 minutes, then run a knife around the edge and turn out onto serving plates.

NUTRITION PER SERVE
Protein 25 g; Fat 55 g; Carbohydrate 20 g; Dietary Fibre 2 g; Cholesterol 255 mg; 2645 kJ (630 cal)

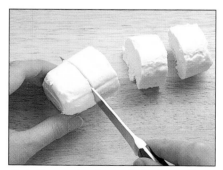

Cut the goats cheese into four slices, using a sharp knife.

Build up layers of potato, prosciutto and goats cheese in the ramekin.

Mix together the sour cream, eggs and cream and pour over the pies.

BARBECUED NEW POTATOES WITH MACADAMIA BUTTER

Preparation time: 30 minutes
Total cooking time: 30–35 minutes
Serves 6

1 kg (2 lb) new potatoes,
    unpeeled, cut into quarters
125 g (4 oz) butter, chopped
150 g (5 oz) honey-roasted
    macadamias
2 tablespoons chopped chives

1 Boil or steam the potatoes until almost tender.

2 Preheat a barbecue grill plate or chargrill pan. Combine the chopped butter, macadamias, chives and some salt and pepper in a food processor. Process in short bursts until the macadamias are finely ground and the mixture is smooth.

3 Lightly grease the preheated barbecue grill or chargrill pan. Cook the potato in batches until lightly blackened and a little crisp on the edges. Cooking the potatoes on the barbecue gives them an unusual smoky flavour. Place the hot potatoes in a large bowl. Add about half of the butter mixture and toss to coat the potatoes. Serve immediately.

NUTRITION PER SERVE
Protein 6 g; Fat 35 g; Carbohydrate 25 g;
Dietary Fibre 4 g; Cholesterol 55 mg;
1845 kJ (440 cal)

COOK'S FILE

Note: It is extremely difficult to make a smaller quantity of the macadamia butter in the food processor. Leftover butter can be refrigerated in an airtight container for up to one month.

Process the butter, nuts, chives and salt and pepper together.

Parboil the potatoes until nearly tender, then barbecue or chargrill.

Mix half the macadamia butter through the potatoes and store the remainder.

POTATO AND HORSERADISH PANCAKES WITH OCEAN TROUT

Preparation time: 40 minutes
+ 20 minutes standing
Total cooking time: 25 minutes
Serves 6 as a starter

1½ cups (185 g/6 oz) self-raising flour
1 teaspoon bicarbonate of soda
1 teaspoon salt
350 ml (11 fl oz) buttermilk
2 eggs, lightly beaten
2½ teaspoons horseradish cream
2½ teaspoons wasabi paste
300 g (10 oz) potatoes, peeled and chopped into large pieces
750 g (1½ lb) ocean trout fillets or salmon fillets
150 ml (5 fl oz) sour cream
125 g (4 oz) butter, for cooking
50 g (1¾ oz) salmon roe
50 g (1¾ oz) black caviar

1 Sift the flour, bicarbonate of soda and salt into a bowl and make a well. Add the buttermilk, eggs and 2 teaspoons each of horseradish and wasabi. Whisk the mixture together until smooth. Cover with plastic wrap and set aside for 20 minutes.
2 Cook the potato in boiling water for 10 minutes. Drain and, when cool enough to handle, grate the potato. Mix with the rested batter.
3 Remove the skin from the trout or salmon and cut the fish into strips.
4 Mix the sour cream with the remaining horseradish and wasabi and refrigerate. Preheat the oven to very slow 120°C (250°F/Gas ½).

5 Melt a little butter in a non-stick frying pan. Add 2 tablespoons of batter and smooth into a neat round shape with the back of a spoon. (When filling the tablespoons, try to be accurate, so the pancakes are all the same size and there is enough for two per serving.) Cook about two or three at a time, over low heat, for about a minute each side, or until golden. Wipe the pan with a paper towel each time, before adding more butter and batter. Transfer the cooked pancakes to an ovenproof plate, cover with a foil and place in the oven to keep warm. Turn off the oven.
6 Melt 30 g (1 oz) of butter in a frying pan. Cook the fish strips in about three batches over medium heat, for 1–2 minutes each side, or until they change colour and are lightly browned. Wipe the pan, add more butter and cook the next batch.
7 To serve, place a pancake into the centre of the plate, spread with a little of the sour cream and arrange the fish strips over the top. Spread a little sour cream on the fish to keep the next pancake in place. Lay the next pancake on top. Spoon about 1 tablespoon of the sour cream over the top and garnish with about a teaspoon each of the salmon roe and black caviar.

NUTRITION PER SERVE
Protein 45 g; Fat 40 g; Carbohydrate 30 g; Dietary Fibre 2 g; Cholesterol 300 mg; 3520 kJ (840 cal)

COOK'S FILE

Note: Wasabi is made from the root of an Asian plant. With its sharp, pungent, fiery taste, it is the Japanese version of horseradish and therefore should be used sparingly. It is available as a paste or dried.

Make a well in the centre of the dry ingredients and pour in the liquid.

Cook the potato for 10 minutes, then cool and grate.

Remove the skin from the trout or salmon and cut into strips.

Mix the sour cream with the remaining horseradish cream and wasabi paste.

Use 2 tablespoons of batter for each pancake. Smooth with the back of a spoon.

Melt the butter in a frying pan and cook the fish in batches.

POPPYSEED AND SALT BREADSTICKS

Preparation time: 25 minutes
Total cooking time: 35 minutes
Serves 4–8

150 g (5 oz) floury potatoes
120 g (4 oz) butter, softened
2 cups (250 g/8 oz) plain flour
1 egg, beaten
poppyseeds and sea salt

1 Preheat the oven to moderately hot 200°C (400°F/Gas 6) and lightly grease two baking trays.
2 Cook the potato in boiling salted water until just tender. Drain and put through a food mill or mash smoothly in a bowl. Add the butter and flour and a little salt, to taste. Mix together to form a rough dough, then knead 10–12 times on a lightly floured surface until soft and smooth.
3 Divide the dough in half. Roll each half out into a rectangle a little larger than 16 x 28 cm (6½ x 11 inches). Trim it down to that size with a sharp knife and cut in half. The trimmings can be re-rolled. Now cut the dough into 1 cm (½ inch) sticks across the width and place on the trays, leaving room to spread. Brush with the beaten egg, sprinkle with poppyseeds and then a little salt. Bake for 10–12 minutes, or until golden.

NUTRITION PER SERVE (8)
Protein 5 g; Fat 15 g; Carbohydrate 25 g; Dietary Fibre 1 g; Cholesterol 60 mg; 1005 kJ (240 cal)

COOK'S FILE

Note: These breadsticks can be kept in an airtight container for up to five days and crisped in the oven.

Mix the potato, butter, flour and a little salt until a rough dough is formed.

Use a sharp knife to cut the dough into 1 cm (½ inch) sticks.

Brush the sticks with beaten egg and then sprinkle with poppy seeds.

POTATO CAKES WITH SMOKED SALMON

Preparation time: 35 minutes
Total cooking time: 15 minutes
Serves 4

1 Lebanese cucumber, finely
   chopped
1 small red onion, finely
   chopped
2 tablespoons capers
1 tablespoon lemon juice
1 teaspoon finely chopped
   lemon thyme or dill
3 tablespoons olive oil
2 eggs

3 tablespoons plain flour
1 tablespoon chopped chives
500 g (1 lb) potatoes, peeled
30 g (1 oz) butter
8–10 thin slices smoked salmon
200 g (6½ oz) thick natural
   yoghurt or sour cream

1 Combine the cucumber, onion, capers, lemon juice, lemon thyme or dill and 1 tablespoon of olive oil in a bowl and season with salt and pepper.
2 Beat the eggs in a large bowl and mix in the flour and chives. Grate the potatoes coarsely into the centre of a tea towel and squeeze tightly in the tea towel to extract as much moisture as possible. Add the potato to the

egg mixture and stir well to combine.
3 Heat the remaining oil with the butter in a large non-stick frying pan and add 2 level tablespoons of potato mixture for each cake. Flatten the cakes to make circles. Cook over low heat, turning once, until golden. Keep warm while cooking the remaining mixture to make 8–10 cakes.
4 Put a slice of salmon on each potato cake and top with a little cucumber mixture and a spoonful of thick yoghurt or sour cream. Garnish with fresh herbs such as dill.

NUTRITION PER SERVE
Protein 25 g; Fat 45 g; Carbohydrate 25 g;
Dietary Fibre 3 g; Cholesterol 205 mg;
2540 kJ (605 cal)

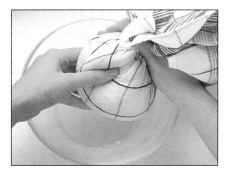

Extract as much moisture as possible from the potatoes by squeezing tightly.

Use two level tablespoons of potato mixture to make each cake.

Turn the cakes once and cook over low heat until golden.

POTATO AND ZUCCHINI TART

Preparation time: 25 minutes
+ 15 minutes refrigeration
Total cooking time: 1 hour 20 minutes
Serves 6

Pastry
1¼ cups (185 g/6 oz) plain flour
125 g (4 oz) chilled butter, cubed
1 egg yolk

Filling
450 g (14 oz) floury potatoes,
    peeled and roughly chopped
⅓ cup (40 g/1¼ oz) plain flour
125 g (4 oz) Jarlsberg cheese,
    grated
⅓ cup (80 ml/2¾ fl oz) cream
2 eggs, separated
2–3 small zucchini, thinly sliced
    lengthways
4 sprigs thyme, to garnish

1 Grease a 25 cm (10 inch) diameter, 2.5 cm (⅛ inch) deep, loose-bottomed flan tin.

2 To make the pastry, put the flour in a bowl with ½ teaspoon of salt. Rub in the butter with your fingertips, until crumbly. Add the egg yolk and 1–2 tablespoons of water, and mix with a knife to form a rough dough. Turn out onto a lightly floured surface and work into a smooth ball, then wrap in plastic wrap and refrigerate for 15 minutes. Preheat the oven to moderately hot 190°C (375°F/Gas 5).

3 On a lightly floured surface, roll out the dough to a circle large enough to fit the prepared tin. Ease the pastry into the tin and trim. Cover with baking paper and fill with rice or dried beans. Bake for 10 minutes and

discard the paper and rice. Bake for another 5–10 minutes.

4 To make the filling, boil or steam the potato until tender. Drain, allow to cool for 5 minutes and mash. Mix in the flour and cheese, stir in ⅔ cup (170 ml/5½ fl oz) of water and when loosely incorporated, add the cream. Whisk until smooth, add the egg yolks and combine well. Season, to taste, with salt and white pepper. Beat the egg whites in a small bowl until

stiff peaks form, fold into the potato mixture and gently pour into the pie crust.

5 Arrange the zucchini over the pie in a decorative pattern. Decorate with thyme and bake for 35–45 minutes, until set and golden brown. Serve slices hot or at room temperature.

NUTRITION PER SERVE
Protein 15 g; Fat 30 g; Carbohydrate 40 g;
Dietary Fibre 3 g; Cholesterol 185 mg;
2105 kJ (500 cal)

Ease the circle of pastry into the prepared tin. The rolling pin can hold the pastry.

Pour the potato mixture into the baked pastry case.

Arrange the thin slices of zucchini over the pie in a decorative pattern.

INDEX

111

INTERNATIONAL GLOSSARY OF INGREDIENTS

capsicum	red or green pepper	fresh coriander	fresh cilantro
eggplant	aubergine	English spinach	spinach
zucchini	courgette	cream	whipping cream
tomato paste (Aus.)	tomato purée, double concentrate (UK)	tomato purée (Aus.)	sieved crushed tomatoes/ passata (UK)

This edition published in 2003 by Bay Books, an imprint of Murdoch Magazines Pty Limited, GPO Box 1203, Sydney NSW 2001, Australia.

Managing Editor: Rachel Carter **Editor:** Wendy Stephen **Food Director:** Jane Lawson **Designer:** Michelle Cutler **Food Editor:** Lulu Grimes **Recipe Development:** Amanda Cooper, Alex Diblasi, Michelle Earl, Joanne Glynn, Lulu Grimes, Michelle Lawton, Barbara Lowery, Sally Parker, Kerrie Ray, Jo Richardson, Alison Turner, Jody Vassallo **Home Economists:** Anna Beaumont, Michelle Lawton, Kerrie Mullins, Justine Poole, Kerrie Ray, Margot Smithyman, Alison Turner **Photographers:** Jon Bader, Ian Hofstetter (cover), Reg Morrison (steps) **Food Stylists:** Amanda Cooper, Michelle Noerianto (cover) **Food Preparation:** Chris Sheppard, Valli Little (cover).
Chief Executive: Juliet Rogers **Publisher:** Kay Scarlett

First printed 1998. This flip edition first published in 2002. Reprinted 2003.
ISBN 1 8977 30 48 9. Printed by Imago Publishing in Thailand.

The nutritional information provided for each recipe does not include any accompaniments, such as rice, unless they are listed in the ingredients. The values are approximations and can be affected by biological and seasonal variations in food, the unknown composition of some manufactured foods and uncertainty in the dietary database. Nutrient data given are derived primarily from the NUTTAB95 database produced by the Australian New Zealand Food Authority.